VITAL SIGNS

VITAL SIGNS

Working Doctors Tell

the Real Story Behind

Medical School & Practice

**Deborah L. Bernal, M.D., with Charles H. Epps III, M.D.,
Peter E. Lavine, M.D., Duane J. Taylor, M.D., and the
Young Physicians Section of the Medical Society
of the District of Columbia**

Peterson's
Princeton, New Jersey

Library of Congress Cataloging-in-Publication Data

Vital signs : working doctors tell the real story about medical school & practice / edited by Deborah L. Bernal, with Charles H. Epps III . . . [et al.].
    p. cm.
  Includes index.
  ISBN 1-56079-376-7
  1. Medicine—Vocational guidance. I. Bernal, Deborah L. II. Epps, Charles H.
  [DNLM: 1. Career Choice—personal narratives. 2. Educational, Medical—United States—personal narratives. W 21 V836 1994]
R690.V55   1994
610.69—dc20
DNLM/DLC
for Library of Congress   94-28687
                                              CIP

Cover and Interior Design by CDS Design

Printed in the United States of America

10 9 8 7 6 5 4 3 2 1

CONTENTS

CONTENTS

C

O

N

T

E

N

T

S

I would like to thank the Medical Society of the District of Columbia's Board of Trustees for their cooperation and support in the completion of this project. Much thanks as well to the Young Physicians Section and its Governing Council—past and present— for lending their insight, dedication, and hard work, not only for this specific project, but for the success of many of our endeavors.

I appreciate the extraordinary efforts of all the contributing authors to this work. Your time and patience were evident in your responses to our many requests over the past months. Most significantly, the donation of your work for the benefit of the Young Physicians Sections' service activities is most commendable. We promise to use the funds wisely in our service and outreach into the community.

I especially want to thank my small, but faithful editorial team, Drs. Charles H. Epps, III, Peter E. Lavine, and Duane J. Taylor, for their persistence throughout the many months of deadlines, status sheets, phone calls, and faxes to our authors and each other. Charles, Peter, and Duane, I appreciate your consistency and endurance.

A very special thank you goes to our Medical Society of D.C. staff member, Shay Thomas. Undoubtedly, without her dedication, organization, and persistence this project could never have been completed in this century! No mere words can express the delight it was working with you on this project (if only I had you to run my life so efficiently!). Your efforts brought the pieces together and kept the rest of us coordinated and focused. You have our heart-felt gratitude.

ACKNOWLEDGMENTS

The Medical Society of the District of Columbia's Young Physicians Section (MSDC-YPS) was formed in 1986. Its goal is to provide a forum for physicians under the age of 40, or in the first five years of professional practice, to foster awareness of their unique needs and concerns, and to ensure continued opportunities to address those needs and concerns.

The MSDC-YPS has been dedicated to community service activities with special emphasis on projects with District of Columbia youth. We are encouraging interest in the health sciences as well as providing health information that is vital to our community. By making ourselves accessible to the youth, we hope to encourage healthy lifestyles, act as role models, or spark an interest in those who have not seriously considered a career in medicine. As a result of these efforts, the Young Physicians Section received the Medical Society of D.C.'s Distinguished Service Award in 1991, for exemplary service to its medical socicty. In 1994, it was recognized by the American Medical Association's Young Physicians Section with a Community Service Award for outstanding efforts in providing health care outreach to community youth.

Vital Signs is being published during a critical time for medicine in the United States—it is the era of health care reform. As a young physician-to-be, just beginning your career, you will be significantly impacted by the changes over the next decade. As advocates for our profession, the MSDC-YPS feel it is important to provide you with a perspective of medicine as a career. We want to help you focus on what motivated you to accept the challenges of becoming a physician and feel comfortable with that choice.

The diversity and flexibility of practice in medicine is one of its strengths. In compiling this book we decided to reflect this by exploring as many aspects of the life of a physician as possible.

And so we begin in Part One, *Choosing a Career in Medicine,* with special essays about the practice of medicine by three seasoned pros who have pursued their careers with vigor: Nancy L. Snyderman, M.D., Medical Correspondent for "Good Morning America," and Associate Clinical Professor of Otolaryngology, California Pacific Medical Center; Benjamin S. Carson Sr., M.D., Director of Pediatric Neurosurgery, The Johns Hopkins Hospital; and LaSalle D. Leffall Jr., M.D., Professor and Chair, Department of Surgery, Howard University. Also included here is a collection of observations by all of the contributors to *Vital Signs,* telling you "Why We Did It."

In Part Two, *Practice Preliminaries,* we present a few essays on such pre-medical concerns as pre-medical school preparations, getting into medical school, and choosing a medical school. We also address two important issues: minorities in medicine and women in medicine.

The Joys of Medical School is the topic of Part Three, and here you'll encounter advice on financing medical school, dealing with life as a medical student, what it's like to be an older medical student, and choosing a residency. What happens after you complete your first four years is covered in Part Four, *Training and Credentialing.* In this section doctors write about postgraduate training, deciding on a specialty, and passing specialty board exams.

In Part Five, *Styles of Practice,* you'll hear from doctors on a variety of topics, including: choosing a location, medicine as a small business, HMOs, public service, and changing careers. Finally, in Part Six, *Reflections,* several doctors consider such issues as volunteerism, medical ethics, and medicine and family life.

A very real and compelling picture emerges from these pages. I hope it is useful to you as you pursue your dream of a career in medicine.

—Deborah L. Bernal, M.D., Chair, Young Physicians Section

CHOOSING A CAREER IN MEDICINE

A Reason to Get Up in the Morning

Nancy L. Snyderman, M.D., Medical
Correspondent, "Good Morning America"
Associate Clinical Professor of Otolaryngology,
California Pacific Medical Center

*"What pulls us to this profession
is an urge to make the human
condition better, a reason to get up
in the morning and face the day,
a desire to look ourselves in the
mirror and know that on this
day we made a person's life
a little bit better."*
—Nancy L. Snyderman, M.D.

CHAPTER 1

I knew I wanted to be a physician when I was in third grade. Now while that may seem awfully early to someone in college who is just now exploring the possibilities of considering medicine—for some of us there didn't seem to be any other options. And I am as convinced now as I was then that this has been the perfect life for me.

My grandfather was a neurologist in rural Texas who considered medicine a calling. My father is 71 and still practicing otolaryngology in Indiana. He must have instilled some magic on his offspring, because both my brother and I followed in his footsteps.

At this point you may be at a crossroads, trying to decide what profession is right for you. While you're trying to decide, the world of medicine has never looked so complicated and perhaps uninviting. But I would like to give you my perspective—not only as a practicing surgeon but as a journalist who has covered the world of medicine for the past eight years. In addition to practicing head and neck cancer surgery in San Francisco, I am also a medical correspondent for ABC News and "Good Morning America." This dual career has given me a unique vantage point for watching changes in medicine, politics, social mores, and societal trends.

No one can deny that there have been huge, and for some people sudden, changes in how medicine is practiced and how everyday people access health care. The center of gravity has shifted: Medicine as my father practiced it in the 1950s and 1960s will never be seen again. And while individual physicians and their academic bodies are scrambling for a piece of the pie, it's important for you to know there will always be a piece for you.

I honestly don't know any doctor who went into medicine for the money or the lifestyle. What pulls us to this profession is an urge to make the human condition better, a reason to get up in the morning and face the day, a desire to look ourselves in the mirror and know that on this day we made a person's life a little bit better.

Governments, hospitals, insurance companies, and physician groups will continue to argue and posture and fight for larger roles, but in the meantime your life revolves around you. No one else. And you have to do what your heart and gut tell you to do. Your head is already leaning toward medicine or you wouldn't be reading this book.

Being paid for your work is important and vital for your survival. And you will make more than enough money to have a handsome life. But your thrills won't come from those insurance checks. They'll come from:

- The woman whose hearing you just restored, who can hear rain on the roof for the first time in years.

- The eleven-year-old who adores you because she is in remission from her leukemia.

- The thirteen-year-old you just talked through her first pap smear.

- The sixty-five-year-old who opens his eyes in the ICU unable to comprehend the miracle that he is alive after heart surgery.

- The eighty-year-old who clutches your hand, uncertain that he wants to live after losing his wife of 55 years.

These are the experiences peculiar to medicine; the memories that linger with you when all the other novelties of the good life have come and gone. These are the memories that beckon us to answer the calling; the memories that on a daily basis reinforce that this is the best way to spend a life.

RESTORING HEALTH

AND HOPE

Benjamin S. Carson Sr. M.D.,

Director of Pediatric Neurosurgery,

The Johns Hopkins Hospital

"For me, the ability to bring a smile to the face of a child and a glimmer of hope to devastated parents is far more rewarding than awards and plaques."

—Benjamin S. Carson Sr., M.D.

As a child I became fascinated with psychiatry because of the images psychiatrists portrayed on various television shows. However, and not surprisingly, when I got to medical school I discovered that psychiatry was extraordinarily different in reality. It wasn't long before I changed course—and chose neurosurgery for my practice.

It is very important for anyone contemplating a career in medicine to gain as clear an understanding as possible about the opportunities available and what is involved in pursuing them. It is for this reason that *Vital Signs* is such an important book—it will give you an insider's look into the many aspects of medicine.

Medicine is extremely challenging intellectually because of the constant changes occurring both in approaches to treatment and the development of new technologies. But, by far the most rewarding aspect of medicine is the unique opportunity and privilege to intervene in situations where patients and their families have been devastated by physical illness or conditions, and to play a significant role in helping restore both health and hope to those families. For me, the ability to bring a smile to the face of a child and a glimmer of hope to devastated parents is far more rewarding than awards, plaques, and media attention. This is not to say that medicine does not provide the successful practitioner with a very comfortable lifestyle. But, for the amount of effort that is needed to pursue a medical career, if one were interested only in comfort, it could be achieved at a much smaller price.

Vital Signs will take you from the process of applying to medical school, through the challenging basic science years, and on into the clinical years. The contributors offer many tips for successfully maneuvering through these stages, as well as advice for completing the internship and residency, and setting up a practice. Seldom has such a comprehensive and thoughtful volume been put together.

EQUANIMITY UNDER DURESS

LaSalle D. Leffall Jr., M.D., F.A.C.S. Professor and Chair, Department of Surgery, Howard University College of Medicine

"Physicians must maintain the degree of tranquility and calmness that will allow them to exercise the best judgment in caring for their patients."

—LaSalle D. Leffall Jr., M.D., F.A.C.S.

CHAPTER 3

After almost a half century in medicine (I entered Howard University College of Medicine in September 1948), I believe that medicine is one of the most noble and honorable professions, because we have the opportunity to help people retain and regain their health—and without health, nothing in life means anything. Thus, it is easy to see why this profession is so satisfying. The expressions of thanks and gratitude that come from satisfied patients make it all worthwhile.

It has been said that to become a physician you must be physically and mentally strong—mentally strong to master the massive amount of information that exists today, and physically strong to keep the long hours often required to care for patients. Maintaining that high standard of surgical discipline, "Equanimity Under Duress," is extremely important. Physicians must achieve the degree of tranquility and calmness that will allow them to exercise their best judgment in caring for patients.

The medical curriculum is a vigorous one, demanding much time and study. You must have a passion for learning—because a career in medicine requires a commitment to excellence, or giving your best and being the best. If there is no *commitment* to excellence, there can be no excellence. As you pursue your medical career, always remember that the patient comes first. A caring, compassionate attitude is essential in providing total care for the patient. So often I am asked by young medical students if they have made the correct choice by studying medicine. My answer to them is a resounding yes, for this profession is as stimulating, demanding, and interesting as it has ever been—and perhaps even more so than before. I enthusiastically recommend this great profession to you.

WHY WE DID IT

The Contributors

"The refuge from pessimism is the good men and women existing at any time in the world—they keep faith and happiness alive."

—Charles E. Norton

W e asked each contributor to this book what motivating factor was behind their desire to become doctors. Here's what they said:

"I am time driven. I chose medicine for my career in the belief — I believe (and, hopefully not smugly) substantiated — that every day's effort would contribute in some way to something worthwhile and larger than myself." — *James R. Hughes, M.D., Pediatrics*

"Life is with people, and as a people-oriented person, medicine offered the opportunity to work with people in a meaningful and profound way. Healer, leader, teacher were words I associated with "doctor." That drew me on." — *Joshua Lipsman, M.D., Family Practice, Public Health, and General Preventive Medicine*

"I enjoy the problem-solving characteristics of the job and the challenges of working with very different people and problems. I wanted a career that I could specifically train for because then I wouldn't have to go through the agony of applying for various jobs, trying to decide what I really wanted to do, and climbing (clawing) up the ladder; In addition, I have always been fascinated with the workings of the body and mind." — *Luette S. Semmes, M.D., Dermatology and Internal Medicine*

"I chose medicine as a career for several reasons: besides allowing me an avenue to make a decent living, medicine allows me to interact with very interesting people with very diverse problems that challenge me intellectually. It is a career I truly enjoy." — *Kevin R. Smith, M.D., Otolaryngology*

"Growing up in a household in which both parents are physicians has been and continues to be a major inspiration." — *Charles H. Epps III, M.D., Ophthalmology*

"At a very young age I was impressed with the vast knowledge of my own family physician. Now I realize acquiring the knowledge was the easy part; it is the wisdom of the art of healing that I will pursue for my lifetime." — *Deborah L. Bernal, M.D., Physical Medicine and Rehabilitation*

"I latched onto and never let go of the idea of becoming a doctor at the tender age of six. As I recall my then six-year-old thoughts, it was because I wanted to be important, to *be* somebody." — *Rodney L. Ellis, M.D., Internal Medicine*

"During high school and college I had developed a deep interest in biological sciences, especially microbiology. Medicine seemed like the best choice to combine a love for pure laboratory science with a more immediate human relevance." — *Peter Hawley, M.D., Anatomic and Clinical Pathology*

"I can't think of another career that is as intellectually challenging and fun, and that allows me to so personally know and help other people. Of course, that's the "intellectualized" view from my present perspective. When I was twenty, I had similar thoughts, but didn't really understand them!" — *Robert I. Keimowitz, M.D., Internal Medicine*

"I was majoring in biochemistry, which I loved, and began to do laboratory research in college, but I was more intrigued by details of the personal lives of my coworkers than by the intricacies of the research itself. I loved science but when I realized that my true interest was people, medicine became the logical career choice." — *Ruth Kevess-Cohen, M.D., Internal Medicine*

"I was working in a hospital in my role of medical technologist doing a research project on a patient who called me "doctor." From that point on I think I wanted to acquire the knowledge so that I could provide the care that this patient was anticipating I could deliver." — *Lawrence S. McDonald, M.D., Internal Medicine*

"I chose medicine because I had a gut feeling to want to help people and particularly those who mentally had gone astray. In my senior year at high school I did a year-long project on the rehabilitation of criminals." — *Edmund Howe, M.D., J.D., Psychiatry*

"I knew since I was six years old that I wanted to be a doctor. I just kept striving toward my goal, not letting anything deter me. I think my determination was so strong that if I encountered any roadblocks, I wouldn't have recognized them anyhow!" — *Caryl G. Mussenden, M.D., Obstetrics and Gynecology*

"What attracted me to a career in medicine? The opportunity to help others and heal with a sense of compassion and service, a strong interest in the sciences, and the diversity of opportunity available. Finally, medicine seemed to provide a means to an end of unselfishly utilizing my God-given talents to perhaps make a difference." — *Duane J. Taylor, M.D., Otolaryngology-Head and Neck Surgery, Facial Plastic and Reconstructive Surgery*

"I had two excellent role models [my parents], who lived and breathed medicine. I never seriously considered anything else." — *Maria L. Chanco Turner, M.D., Dermatology*

"When I first considered medical school, I did so knowing that the continually changing face of medicine would offer a lifetime of intellectual challenge that I craved." — *Martin W. Gallagher, Jr., M.D., Internal Medicine*

"I've always had good interpersonal skills and medicine allowed me to combine my love for people with my scientific and analytical curiosity. The exposure of growing up in a medical family allowed me to appreciate how clinical knowledge and skills could be applied to help others. Medicine is a very emotionally, intellectually, and spiritually gratifying profession." — *Peter E. Lavine, M.D., Orthopedic Surgery*

"I like science and I like people. Back in the 7th and 8th grades, I recall wanting to "mix" the two and the idea of being a physician seemed to fit the bill best. Some of my friends laughed at the idea and thought I couldn't do it. So, I decided to take this on as a challenge and prove them wrong: I'm still smiling!" — *Catherine L. Salem, M.D., Radiology and Oncology*

"I wanted to become a physician because I wanted to improve the health of the population by influencing large populations of public and private healthcare systems." — *Lisa Egbounu-Davis, M.D., Pediatrics*

"I became a physician because of my interest in science, and wanting to be of help to people." — *William K. Payne II, M.D., Pediatrics*

"Though I was very interested in many of the life sciences, when it came to deciding on my career it was the unhesitating, absolute desire to become a doctor. I believed that no other career gave as much opportunity to help people as much as being a doctor. I knew very early in life that as a doctor I could look back on my life, one day, with great pride knowing that I had made a difference in people's lives." — *J. Kevin Belville, M.D., Ophthalmology*

"I had a great role model, an aunt in Detroit who was a doctor. I was always encouraged in school by interested teachers to "live up to my potential" because I received good grades in math and science. But I also felt a great desire to do something that involved helping people directly, hands-on. So being a physician seemed like a good combination, and my aunt was my motivation that it could be done." — *Renee R. Jenkins, M.D., Pediatrics*

"My earliest memories are those of administering medications and care to relatives who were ill, and coming to a realization that I believed I had a talent for comforting and making those who were ill feel better . . . but also, wanting to do 'research' to help find cures for their diseases so they would not suffer or die. And so, by age 4, I knew I wanted to be a physician. Amazingly, considering that this was in the 1940s when there were few women doctors, no one told me that there were any reasons why I could not become a doctor if I studied and worked hard to do so!" — *Vivian W. Pinn, M.D., Pathology*

"My academic studies were very important to me. In high school I became very interested in science, and at the same time, I was involved with the high school band. I ended up choosing science as my profession but never made light of the music which I also took very seriously. I was extremely proud to be a physician. Through my medicine, I had achieved a great deal. I had overcome the poverty of Southwest Louisiana and was part of a discipline which had been passed down from generations of scientists and scientific advancement."—*Cleve Francis Jr., M.D., Cardiology*

"My father was ill for several years during my childhood. The fact that my family didn't know what was wrong with him probably drew me into a career in medicine. That, plus the fact that I was very interested in science."—*Ronald H. Tinsley, M.D., Otolaryngology*

PRACTICE

PRELIMINARIES

Setting Your Sights on Medicine: Pre-Med Preparations

Deborah L. Bernal, M.D.

"To make preparations does not spoil the trip."

—Guinea Proverb

Since the career of medicine is one that embraces life-long learning (it's the only way physicians can keep abreast of the latest medical information), medical schools are most interested in candidates who display the commitment and motivation for continuous learning. To distinguish yourself, you must consistently stay motivated for peak performance: performing well academically and challenging yourself through involvement in extracurricular activities.

THE IMPORTANCE OF UNDERGRADUATE EDUCATION

Although there is no specific undergraduate major required for admission to medical school, most schools require one year of physics, organic chemistry, inorganic chemistry, and biology, each with its related laboratory work. Equally valued, however, is a broad education—one that has emphasized course work in communications, the humanities, and the social sciences. In fact, acceptance into medical school according to an undergraduate major has varied over the years. There are times when nonscience majors have fared better than both physical and biological science majors—and times when they have not. [The Association of American Medical Colleges (AAMC) publishes an annual report, "Trends in Medical School Applicants and Matriculates," that summarizes all demographics.]

Since you can't foresee the future and guess next year's popular major, what will put you in good stead as a desirable candidate with the school of your choice are the quality and depth of your education, the sense of purpose you bring to your undergraduate life, and well-developed interpersonal skills. This makes each course—and instructor—you choose an important decision. Try to take some key classes from noted professors and make an effort to know them: ask well-thought-out questions, visit them during their office hours, and try to get involved with their research projects. If you establish a good working relationship, they could become sources for letters of recommendation.

Always go to class, study regularly, prepare for lectures, and avoid cramming for exams. Equally important: avoid distractions, allow for rest periods, and exercise.

Since it's important for your academic record to show diversity, choose electives that will stimulate your interest as well as boost your grade point average.

STAYING MOTIVATED

It's difficult to stay motivated and focused on your studies with all the exciting activities—on and off campus—that interest you. Two of the most effective ways I know for maintaining self-discipline are:

- finding a mentor and identifying a role model
- doing more than just attending class and studying

A mentor is someone you know and respect for their knowledge and wisdom, who becomes a counselor to you. The mentor you choose could be a peer, upperclassmate, professor, relative, or friend. He or she will have the experience you lack, and from that provide insight into your goal.

A role model can be anyone (actually, you can have more than one role model) who possesses the positive qualities you need in order to achieve your goal. Unlike a mentor, with whom you engage in a relationship, you don't have to know your role model—he or she can be living or dead, historical or fictional—as long as their experience can strengthen your resolve.

For as long as I can remember, I have been fascinated with medicine. I was initially impressed by the doctor who cared for me as a toddler when I developed pneumonia. In junior high, I was intrigued by the specimen of a human fetus my teacher brought to class for us to observe—it was then I set my sights on a career in medicine. Today, I continue my journey with the assistance of my mentors and role models.

In addition to helping you become a well-rounded individual, extracurricular activities can also stimulate motivation. Finding a summer job or program can augment and strengthen your academic record. If you can't find a medical job, you might consider volunteering at a hospital or clinic. Be careful, though: Quality is more important than quantity. Don't spread yourself too thin. Showing dedication and leadership is more meaningful than being a member of a long list of affiliations. Also, balance your work/study life with outside activities. Finding an outlet for your creative instincts will also help sharpen your resolve.

Planning and action are the keys to success in any endeavor. I truly believe if you focus your thoughts and energies toward achieving your goals, you can get there from here.

Making the Cut: Getting Into Medical School

Robert I. Keimowitz, M.D.

"Knowledge is like a garden—if it is not cultivated, it cannot be harvested."

—Guinea Proverb

$\mathbf{Y}$ou are pursuing a noble, exciting, challenging, and very reward-ing career. That's not to say that being a doctor is an easy job, or that every day and every patient will bring you satisfaction and fulfillment. However, can you think of another field that allows you to be challenged with fascinating science, be reasonably rewarded, while always serving someone in need?

BEGIN AT THE BEGINNING

It all starts with the application process. There is a variety of rich resources available to applicants. Don't hesitate to contact your col-lege's career and/or preprofessional office, which should have a library of resource materials. Among the many commercial publications avail-able is a singular resource called *Medical School Admissions Require-ments* (MSAR), published annually by the Association of American Medical Colleges (AAMC). I consider this a "must have" resource, and strongly recommend that you buy your own copy. In addition to detailed information submitted by each school about its curriculum and admissions policies, this directory also includes excellent general in-formation about the admissions process. The data are accurate and up-to-date.

The number of applications submitted to medical schools nation-ally varies greatly over time. The most fundamental determinant is the number of 22-year-olds who will graduate from college that particular year. Other influences play substantial roles, including the economy, the news, and public discussion of the profession. Over the past three decades, the number of medical school applications peaked in 1974, plummeted to a nadir in 1987, and since then have increased substan-tially. In the applicant pool for the class that entered in 1993, there were more than 2.5 applicants for every space in an American medical school. Although this figure is very high, it fails to have the "punch" of school-specific data: for example, the class entering The George Washington University School of Medicine and Health Sciences in the fall of 1994, had more than 12,500 applicants for 150 spaces! (These data also indicate that applicants apply to a substantial number of schools.)

The number of applications/applicants also varies significantly by region, with the majority of applicants coming from the two coasts. Some states, for instance California, have a very high ratio of applicants to spaces reserved for in-state students; others, for instance the Central states, have relatively few resident applicants. These numbers affect the competitiveness of those schools. And while preference for in-state residents is typical of state institutions, private schools are not free from considerations of applicants' states of residence. For example, a number of private schools annually receive substantial sums of money based on the number or percent of in-state students who matriculate. This support must strongly influence the decisions of admissions committees. Only a few private schools receive essentially no support from their state; therefore, they have less of an obligation to accept state residents.

THE APPLICATION PROCESS

Applying to medical school became considerably easier in the past two decades because of the introduction of a centralized application service, organized and administered by the AAMC. In 1994, the vast majority of U.S. medical schools participated in the American Medical College Application Service (AMCAS), whereby applicants complete a single application and submit it to AMCAS. The application requires a fair amount of demographic information, a detailed listing of all the courses you have taken after completing high school, your grades in each of these courses, and a personal statement—an essay on a topic of your choosing.

Once AMCAS has all the necessary documents—including Medical College Admissions Test (MCAT) results—the application is collated, grades are verified, and yearly averages and cumulative grade points are calculated. Then AMCAS reproduces and distributes this information to each school that you designate. Your fee is determined by the number of schools to which you apply.

Some schools start processing applications immediately on receipt of the materials from AMCAS; others request a secondary, or school-specific, supplemental application and an application fee. (Obviously then, before you submit your AMCAS application, you should have done enough research to be sure that you have *completed* your application. Otherwise, you are simply wasting time and money!) Schools will then ask you to also submit letters of recommendation. A small percent of applicants will subsequently be invited for an interview.

WHAT ARE MEDICAL SCHOOLS LOOKING FOR?

Given the number of applicants per position in U.S. schools, admission committees look for something distinct in each applicant. This doesn't mean you must be top in your class academically—there are many areas of achievement and endeavor that schools consider. It is appropriate here to remind you of some principles by which most admission officers operate. First, most believe that actions are more important than words. Thus, rather than just reading your statement about concern for others, they will look for evidence of that trait in your application or letters of recommendation. Second, most believe that the best predictor of future performance is past performance in a similar situation.

The following are factors considered by virtually all medical schools:

- *Grades.* The academic work of medical school isn't difficult conceptually (and certainly the high-level science courses you took in college are at least as demanding), but the volume of material you are expected to assimilate in short periods of time is *enormous.* Nothing could be more absurd than equating performance in organic chemistry with the likelihood of becoming a good doctor. Nonetheless, a strong performance in difficult courses, especially those requiring a fair amount of memorization, is often regarded as predictive of getting through years one and two of medical school. And you can't become a physician if you can't satisfactorily pass the basic courses! In general, medical schools seem to weigh science and math grades more than "all other" grades (as defined by AMCAS). But schools treat grades differently: Some won't consider an applicant with less than a 3.4 average; others set a floor (often around 3.0), but look for additional qualities to differentiate among their applicants.

- *MCAT Scores.* Since medical schools have difficulty comparing their applicants' academic prowess with grades alone, the MCAT science scores tend to be used as an equalizing measure across colleges. The reading scores give the admissions committee some sense of your ability to assimilate from a written passage. Recognizing that many universities don't teach students to develop good writing skills, and believing that these skills are required for physicians to communicate clearly with one another about their patients, a writing sample was introduced to the MCAT a few years ago. The two required essays are rated and this writing score seems to be getting some attention by selection committees, particularly in situations where the decision is close.

■ *Letters of Recommendation.* Even the term "recommendation" tells you about the shortcomings of what should ideally be "letters of evaluation." Few, if any, students have even negatively tinged comments submitted. Nonetheless, all schools ask for recommendations, and while assessing whether you walk on water and only get your soles (versus your ankles!) wet, the admissions committees try to learn something new and influential about you from those sources. In general, it is wise to get a letter from your college's premedical advisory committee since it is likely to be balanced, more critical, and is generally afforded more weight in the decision process. It is also helpful to get at least one letter from someone who knows you very well, and who often has a great deal of contact with young people. Someone who has been isolated from college students and medical school applicants for a number of years may lack a frame of reference, and so his or her letter will not be seen as informative as one from your university's chaplain, for example. Finally, while state schools may need to be responsive to political leaders, at many schools a letter from your congressperson may imply more about parental contributions than about the strength of the applicant.

■ *Other Considerations.* Medical schools vary greatly in how they weigh the variables they consider. State schools often use grades and the MCAT as the predominant variables, while private schools are more likely to consider other qualities as well. For example, some schools value research activity and publications; others focus on recruiting people likely to go into primary care careers, and so look for evidence of an affinity to rural lifestyles and commitment to primary care specialties. Some schools are particularly interested in seeing service to others or leadership qualities, and look not for a list of extracurricular groups that a student joined, but for evidence of activity, commitment, and leadership in one or more groups.

The role your undergraduate school has on your acceptance tends to be school-specific, but virtually all medical schools are comfortable with particular pre-med advisors, or have a particularly positive response to a few specific colleges, based on the strengths of students from those schools who did particularly well in medical school. In general, go to the best school you can! But watch out for schools with very high rates of medical school acceptance: they often achieve those percentages by refusing to endorse anyone who doesn't have high grades and MCAT scores.

Your college major rarely determines a committee's decision. Some schools believe that students with considerable college science have an easier time making the transition to medical school, and therefore favor such students. Others think that breadth of education is, in the long run, best for future physicians, and tend to overselect nonscience majors. For a number of years, the percentage of students accepted to medical school varied somewhat by students' majors. The majors that had the highest percentage of students accepted to medical school in 1992–93 were interdisciplinary studies and philosophy: In both, more than 60 percent of applicants were accepted, whereas 43.5 percent of zoology majors were accepted. However, without question, the major most frequently represented in medical students is zoology. My advice is that you major in a subject you really enjoy and want to learn a great deal about, while recognizing that you will be exposed to a great deal of science in medical school.

THE INTERVIEW

Schools vary greatly in their reliance and use of interviews in the selection process. A few have abandoned interviews, recognizing that they are not predictive of students' subsequent performance in medical school. However, most use the interview to get a better sense of applicants' comfort with themselves, and their ability to make contact and engage in intelligent conversation with a stranger.

The topics covered in an interview are as different as the medical schools to which you can apply. However, it is likely that medical schools will try to assess your knowledge and views about major issues confronting the profession. And these days, one issue likely to be invoked is health care reform. With medicine and health care heading into unchartered waters, and with "the experts" predicting that the profession will change greatly, you had better be conversant about the changes likely to occur and ready to present your views clearly.

The interview is very important from *your* point of view. Not only does it give you a chance to see each school's physical plant, but much more importantly, it often reveals a good deal about the school, its students' culture and style, and the strengths and weaknesses of its educational program.

HOW CAN I DISTINGUISH MYSELF?

This is not a question to ask in the year you begin the application process! The year in which you apply is the time for filling "holes," not for "re-creating" yourself. Indeed, admissions committees tend to be sensitive and sometimes a bit skeptical about the perfectly oriented and prepared student.

Rather than trying to find a cookie-cutter mold to fit into, my advice is allow yourself to follow your interests and invest yourself in one or two activities that you really like, and that you think will help you grow and develop into the person *you'd* like to be. It is not at all surprising that admissions committees like people who like themselves.

There is little question that medical schools are trying to redress historical problems, and seek students from minority groups currently underrepresented in the medical field. African Americans, American Indians, Mexican Americans, and mainland Puerto Ricans are so defined by the AAMC. Students from those backgrounds—with strong interest in and aptitude for the study of medicine—will find medical schools quite receptive to them.

HOW CAN I BE SURE MEDICINE IS FOR ME?

This is without question the most difficult and the most important question you can ask. There is no set answer. Most schools do think it is appropriate for you to have a personal sense of what medicine is about, but they differ greatly in how to assess that. Some almost demand that you have worked in a medical area. Others—from my perspective, quite correctly—look for a legitimate basis for your interest, but also recognize that a semester or summer in an emergency room is no guarantee that you will have gained a reasonable perspective on the career. Whatever way you use to try to assess your interest, be sure you can explain it fully.

Admission to medical school is important, but should not control your academic and personal development. You must not let this process derail your education, your sense of self-direction, or your integrity. And, since an admissions system worth anything will be attuned to unsubstantiated "fluff," be yourself. Put yourself forward in the most positive manner with which you are comfortable, but recognize that there is an element of randomness and imprecision in the selection process. If you are accepted, wonderful! If you are not, you can certainly review your application, background, and weaknesses, and try to address them. Finally, you must recognize that there are other ways in which you can live, be productive, and help others outside of the medical profession.

Challenge 2000:

Minorities in

Medicine

Kevin R. Smith, M.D., and

Duane J. Taylor, M.D.

"Excellence of performance will transcend the barriers of racial discrimination and segregation."

—Charles R. Drew, M.D.

CHAPTER 7

Although it is not adequately reflected in most historical literature, this country's racial, ethnic, and cultural diversity has contributed
significantly to the progress of medicine and science. One can only
imagine the scores of lives that would have been lost had Dr. Charles
Drew not discovered the method for preserving blood and blood
products for eventual transfusion. In more recent years, Drs. Antonia
Novello and M. Joycelyn Elders became the first Hispanic and African-
American physicians, respectively, to serve as Surgeon General of the
United States. However, despite the outstanding contributions of these
and other minority physicians, the percentage of minorities working in
medicine is still quite small.

The 1990 census estimated that African-Americans accounted for
only 3.7 percent of physicians in the U.S. while comprising approximately 11.7 percent of the population. Hispanics, the second largest
minority group in the U.S. (9% of the population) only accounted for 4.9
percent of the physicians. Native Americans comprised 0.7 percent of
the population and only 0.1 percent of physicians. Including mainland
Puerto Ricans, these groups comprised 19.4 percent of the population,
but account for only 10.4 percent of applicants to medical school. In
fact, the only group doing well are Asians. According to the Association
of American Medical Colleges (AAMC), Asians are not an underrepresented minority in the medical field. Despite comprising only 1.8
percent of the population, they account for 11.8 percent of the physicians.

A HISTORY OF MINORITIES IN MEDICAL SCHOOL

Prior to the 1970s, segregated institutions played an important role
in limiting the number of minorities who could attend medical school. In
fact, between the 1920s and 1960s, African-Americans were the largest
minority group attending American medical schools, yet only comprised approximately 3 percent of students. Most minority students
attended one of the two predominantly black medical schools—Howard
University College of Medicine in Washington, D.C., and Meharry
Medical College in Nashville. Within the past decade, two more

predominantly black medical schools were founded, providing minority students a greater choice in medical education: Morehouse School of Medicine, in Atlanta, and Charles R. Drew University of Medicine and Science, in Los Angeles.

In 1968, AAMC set a goal to increase the number of underrepresented minority students in medical school in order to reflect their respective percentages of the U.S. population. As a result, between 1968 and 1975, minority enrollment increased by nearly 1,200—from 3 percent to 10 percent of all first-year students. Enrollment decreased slightly in the 1980s, but has begun to catch up in the 1990s. In 1992, first-year underrepresented minorities represented 12 percent of all students, still falling short of population parity, which nationally is 19.4 percent.

PRE-MEDICAL PREPARATIONS

As a minority student in college considering medical school, take advantage of opportunities to prepare yourself. Many medical schools throughout the country offer summer programs for minority college students. These programs are usually designed to expose you to the medical school environment early, enrich and strengthen pre-medical knowledge, and prepare you for the application process. Every U.S. medical school has a contact person primarily responsible for minority affairs who can provide specific information about the availability and requirements of these programs (see the 1993–94 AAMC *Publication, Trends in Medical School Applicants and Matriculants*). Pre-medical counselors or advisors at your undergraduate school also may prove helpful.

Also be aware that the National Institutes of Health sponsors biomedial research opportunities for underrepresented minorities. These opportunities are not only valuable experiences, but will make you an even stronger applicant for medical school. (See Appendix A at the end of the book.)

Make an effort to talk to minority students currently enrolled in the medical school, as well as each school's minority affairs contact person, and ask the following questions:

1. What is the track record of acceptance, retention, and graduation of underrepresented minority students in your school?

2. Are there underrepresented minority faculty members?
3. What academic and personal support systems are in place?
4. Are there financial aid resources available specifically for under-represented minority students?
5. How do minority students from the medical school fare in obtaining residency slots of their choice?

The answers you receive may or may not be relevant to you. For some, being one of a few minority students may not matter—it is an acceptable challenge. Others may find the idea of attending a predominantly minority institution most appealing. Several physicians who have attended these schools indicate that there are unique advantages and strengths like camaraderie, support, and abundance of minority role models. One concern mentioned by some students is that these schools may not be as well recognized, when pursuing future postgraduate training, research, faculty positions, and employment. Ultimately, however, the institution you choose to attend should be one that provides the best environment to assure your successful completion and solidly prepares you for your chosen path in medicine.

LIFE IN MEDICAL SCHOOL

You must acquire a tough mental attitude that will allow you to survive and excel in a stressful and sometimes uncomfortable environment. At any point during your training you could encounter insensitive stereotypical attitudes. Dr. Smith reflects on one such experience he had:

My roommate in medical school was white. One day he expressed a conviction that medical schools do an injustice to minorities by using lower standards for admission; he said he respected white physicians more because he felt they *earned* their degrees. In a flash, I responded, saying that there is no way to determine what his or any student's credentials were—white or minority—and that since no "minority exams" or "white exams" are administered by medical schools, minority students who pass the exams and finish medical school deserve the same respect as any other student. After a pause and some reasonable thought, my roommate recanted his statement.

If you commonly encounter racial or ethnic statements, jokes, or unjustified evaluations, it is helpful to keep a diary of these occurrences so that, if necessary, they can be presented with documented facts, rather than vague recollections.

The search for and identification of role models is important and can make life easier from the time you start to think about medicine as a career to the completion of your training. Minority faculty members and community physicians can prove to be invaluable mentors, helping you gain confidence with the realization that someone else from your racial or ethnic background has successfully completed the challenge you are facing. Also take the time to seek out minority upperclasspeople—they may prove to be your most valuable source of support and insight. Participation in local and national medical societies (for example, National Medical Student Association, Association of American Indian Physicians, or National Medical Association) also can serve as a valuable source of support.

The AAMC has again targeted the underrepresented minorities with a new endeavor: "Project 3000 by 2000." Its goal is to nearly double the numbers of underrepresented minorities entering medical schools by the year 2000. By creating alliances with universities, the project hopes to cultivate, identify, and retain students throughout this education pipeline, so that by the year 2000 there will be at least 3,000 underrepresented minority students entering medical school.

CHOOSING A MEDICAL SPECIALTY

In your final year of medical school you'll select and compete for residency training programs in an area of specialization. The competition for these positions varies, depending on the area of specialty. Studies have shown a declining interest in primary care fields and an increasing interest in medical specialties among all medical students.

In 1987, the American Medical Association conducted a survey of minority physicians younger than 40 years old and in practice less than seven years. They found that less than half of the 5,865 respondents were in primary care. Despite this, African-Americans and Hispanics still had higher proportions going into primary care than any other group: at 44 percent and 45 percent respectively. Only 38 percent of white physicians were in primary care. With the exception of African-Americans, the most common nonprimary care fields for physicians were medicine and surgery subspecialties. The most common specialties for young African-American physicians were internal medicine and obstetrics and gynecology. Another interesting finding of this study was that minority physicians were more likely to serve members of their own race.

A multitude of social, economic, and cultural factors impact on our health care system and its delivery: Minority communities around the country are trying to cope with AIDS, infant mortality, certain types of cancer, and community violence. These are areas in which a minority physician with a unique sensitivity toward his or her minority group as a provider, community leader, patient advocate, and role model can make a difference. Although all aspects of medicine, from practice and research to teaching and public health, are in need of underrepresented minority physicians, it may be that your greatest reward will be to give back in service to your community.

KEEPING YOUR EYES ON THE PRIZE

It is important that, while on the road toward a successful career, you don't isolate yourself. Pre-medical studies, medical school, and residency training are completed with the greatest personal fulfillment and least amount of pain if you learn to study, interact, and work with your classmates—regardless of their race or cultural background. Isolating yourself can cause you to miss out on important study sessions, exam preparation, and obtaining important information about available career opportunities.

As a practicing minority physician, you will probably be confronted with obstacles and challenges that confront other underrepresented minorities in society. Depending on the location and area of specialty, your patients may or may not be primarily from your minority group: Remember, since our numbers are disproportionately low, patients within and outside of your minority group may find having a minority doctor a new experience. This may require patience on both sides of the doctor-patient relationship.

You also may find breaking into the network of referring physicians in your area a challenge, in spite of your qualifications. Although it will require some extra effort, as well as reliance on other minority physicians, it will be worth it.

There will always be those who will distract you, questioning your ability, motivation, and determination. However, if you only listen to those who encourage, motivate, and teach you—and keep your "eyes on the prize"—you will attain your goal.

BEWARE THE GLASS CEILING: WOMEN IN MEDICINE

Vivian W. Pinn, M.D.

"For a variety of reasons, women have been denied the opportunity to contribute their share, in accordance with their potential."

—Benazir Bhutto

CHAPTER 8

This statement was made several years ago by the Prime Minister of Pakistan Benazir Bhutto about women's health and economic development in third world countries, but it could easily be applied to the history of women in the medical sciences in this country. However, change is occurring, and significant strides in the participation of women in all aspects of careers in medicine are beginning to be in evidence.

While there are increased opportunities for women in medicine, women must be aware of the full range of career options and effective ways to be successful in reaching their chosen goals. Women are needed as practitioners in all medical specialties, but also as teachers, administrators, deans, researchers, and policymakers. Women can enjoy the success and personal contentment that the medical profession can provide. In addition to maximizing their attributes and abilities, it is important to take advantage of the many existing support systems and counsel providing guidance to all those who wish to enter, and succeed, in medicine.

CURRENT STATUS OF WOMEN IN MEDICINE

It was not too long ago that a woman would find herself to be the only, or one of few, women in her medical school class, residency program, or in the practice of medicine in her community. However, women are now encountering many more women colleagues of diverse racial and ethnic backgrounds in their classrooms, practice groups, and specialties.

While women were only 7.6 percent of physicians in the United States in 1970, they represented 18.1 percent of physicians in 1992. It is projected that 30 percent of all physicians will be women by 2010.[1] This should not be surprising as women represent 45 percent of all civilian workers in the American labor force (although they have continued to be underrepresented in science and engineering).[2]

In 1969, only 9.4 percent of all applicants to medical school were women (2,289).[3] This number rose to 10,400 by 1987. Since 1987, there has been a 70 percent increase in applications from women: in 1993, 17,944 women were applicants for the total of 16,000 first-year medical school positions.[4] Of those admitted to medical school in the entering class of 1993, 42 percent were women. Women constituted 61 percent of Black and 45 percent of other underrepresented minorities who were new entrants in this class.[5] According to the American Association of Medical Colleges (AAMC) in 1992–93, more than 50 percent of the entering classes were women at 18 U.S. medical schools. Women are now 40.3 percent of all medical students in this country; this means that a total of 26,854 women will be entering the physician work force within the next four years.[6]

Although at one time women found that their choices of residency or postgraduate training were limited to a few specialties, today women have their choice of almost any specialty they desire. Women are now 20 percent of residents in general surgery,[7] and they are entering other surgical subspecialties in more significant numbers. In 1992, women received 9.3 percent of positions in neurosurgery, 8.4 percent in orthopedics, and 6.8 percent in urology.[8] Women are also entering in greater numbers such fields as pathology, anesthesiology, radiology, and dermatology.

In 1991, about one-third of women in graduate medical education programs were training in internal medicine and pediatrics. Obstetrics/ gynecology (OBGYN), family practice, and psychiatry accounted for 26 percent of women residents[9]; in 1992 over 54 percent of all new residents in OBGYN, almost 65 percent of new pediatric residents, and 75 percent of those entering preventive medicine programs were women.[10]

More women physicians have chosen careers in internal medicine, pediatrics, and general practice, in that order, followed by psychiatry, OBGYN, anesthesiology, and pathology. While the numbers of women are greater in internal medicine, women are the majority of pediatricians.[11]

As a result of increasing numbers of women in general surgery residency programs, the numbers have grown from only 1 percent of those in practice in 1990, to more than 6 percent, with a projection of women constituting 10 percent by 2000.[12] And, in spite of higher retirement rates for female physicians, their expected work lives are similar to male physicians because of women's lower mortality rates.[13]

Of the 125,782 women physicians in the United States, the great majority (107,898) are involved in patient care, including office- or hospital-based practices, as residents, full-time hospital staff, and clinical fellows. Medical teaching, administration, research, or other activities constitute the major professional activity for another 6,880 female physicians.[14]

ACADEMIC MEDICINE AND BIOMEDICAL RESEARCH

Women on U.S. medical school faculties are increasing in numbers, but are still lagging in advanced or tenured faculty appointments. Of the total faculty in 1993, 23.5 percent were women.[15] Of the 17,642 women faculty members, only 16.1 percent are nonwhite. Although over 56 percent of males are in senior positions (professor or associate professor), only 28.2 percent of females have been promoted to these positions. Over 49 percent of women (vs. 34.8 percent of men) are at the assistant professor rank, with almost 19 percent as instructors, in contrast to only 7.8 percent of men at this level. And, women are more often on nontenure academic tracks in clinical departments than are men.[16]

The number of women who have been appointed as a chair of a medical school department has slowly increased, but women still are only about 4 percent of all chairs.[17] The majority of women chairs are in microbiology, pediatrics, and family or community medicine. There are no women chairs of medical school departments of surgery and internal medicine. The top academic leadership position in the 126 U.S. medical schools have only slowly yielded to women. As of early 1994, there are only three women deans: Dr. Nancy Gary at the Uniformed Services University of the Health Sciences School of Medicine; Dr. Nilda Candelario of the University of Puerto Rico School of Medicine; and Dr. Paula Stillman of the Eastern Virginia Medical School.

With expanding horizons in biotechnology and science, there is a need for more women to participate in investigations that will open new frontiers of knowledge about health, disease, and scientific technology. While exact figures are not available for those who are participating in research careers, it is recognized that there is a need to increase not only the number of women who are biomedical and behavioral investigators, but also the number of women who are in policymaking positions that can influence or determine the direction of research initiatives.

The amount of research dollars awarded to women for competing and noncompeting grants from the National Institutes of Health (NIH), for example, has quadrupled between fiscal years 1982 and 1991.[18] Women and men have equal success rates for competing research grants, but women submitted, and received, only 19 percent of the total. While this is encouraging progress, efforts are being made to increase the number of women who do apply for funding and to increase their ability to successfully compete for research awards.

WOMEN'S HEALTH AND WOMEN IN BIOMEDICAL CAREERS

Women's gaps in knowledge about women's health, research related to women's health, and access and delivery of health care to women have become issues of national concern. Many women's health advocates, women physicians, and members of Congress have expanded this concern to the inclusion of women's health, beyond the traditional OBGYN, in medical school curricula and advanced medical education. Health care reform has also called attention to diseases of women and the health care they receive.

This new focus on women's health issues has heightened attention beyond the inclusion of women's health within medical school curricula, to the recruitment, retention, and advancement of women in medical and biomedical careers.

Recognizing the actual and potential contribution of women to the advancement of scientific knowledge, as well as in the delivery of health care, is a priority today. Many are convinced that the best means of ensuring that research related to women's health remains a visible and active priority as we enter the twenty-first century, and to ensure that women's health care is addressed with gender-specific knowledge, sensitivity, and caring, is to increase the number of women in medicine as well as in advanced and policymaking positions in research institutions—including universities, medical schools, the federal government, and the private sector.

By no means does this mean that only women can do effective research on women's health issues or that all research is invalid unless women have directed it, or that all health care for women must be provided by women. However, many believe that there is a direct relationship between the amount—and quality—of research being conducted on women's health issues and the number of women engaged in this research.

OVERCOMING BARRIERS TO CAREERS IN MEDICINE

A number of general issues and barriers have been identified that are common to women considering, or who have entered, the medical profession regardless of race, ethnic or cultural background, or specialty.[19-21] These are:

- recruitment of women

- role models and mentors—visibility of women in medicine

- career paths and rewards

- reentry after maternity leave

- the dual role of women as parents and income earners

- sexual discrimination and sexual harassment

- research initiatives on women's health

- sensitizing men about women's career matters

- minorities and racial discrimination

Also of concern is the role of networking, professional organizations, and government in encouraging and providing support for women in biomedical careers.

Recruiting women into biomedical careers is a major need, which is often thwarted by gender stereotyping, especially in career counseling. Even young women who demonstrate an aptitude and interest in science are frequently discouraged from pursuing a science or medical career by parents or educators. Gender role stereotyping appears to most seriously affect minority girls. Yet, the continuing increase of women in the applicant pool and in the entering classes of medical school seems to indicate that this barrier is no longer significantly preventing women from seeking, and achieving, careers in medicine.

Role models and mentoring are important factors in recruiting women into careers in medicine. The paucity of role models, especially women role models, is a serious barrier to all career phases of women in science and medicine. Seeing mostly men in high-ranking positions in medicine subtly reinforces the notion that women do not belong in medicine or research careers.

A lack of role models implies a lack of mentors: women who can personally guide and encourage other women in their careers. Mentors form a fundamental rung in the career ladder of medicine. Without mentoring, women may be disadvantaged in obtaining research grants, publication opportunities, tenure-track positions, and other opportunities to enhance their careers. As you consider medicine as a career, or even after you have entered the profession, you should identify, select, and appeal to appropriate mentors to guide and advise you in your efforts.

CAREER PATHS

Like other fields, medicine does have a career glass ceiling, which the increased participation and leadership of women in medicine are beginning to shatter. The wage gap between men and women physicians has not been eliminated, and, in many instances, you may receive less compensation than your male colleagues.[22]

Sexual discrimination and sexual harassment are often described as being widespread in medicine and in scientific institutions. As an example, in interviews for medical school or postgraduate positions, you may be asked about plans for having families three times as often as men. (This is, of course, an illegal question.)

One of the questions most asked by women who were considering medicine as a career in the 1960s is still the most common question asked today: Can women have marriage, family, and a successful career in medicine? The answer is yes, but there may be difficulties to overcome and sacrifices to be made. Although there are many, many examples of women who have effectively managed families and careers, there are still issues to be resolved about the dual role of a woman as professional and wife, mother, and caretaker.

Unfortunately, the medical profession does not fully accommodate the pregnancy and parenting responsibilities of women, and often penalizes those professional women who choose to have families through inflexible time restrictions on advancement, fellowship opportunities, and tenure. Nearly 50 percent of all U.S. medical programs have no written maternity leave policy. Only 37.5 percent of medical schools have formal maternity leave, only 50 percent of all teaching hospitals have child-care facilities for physicians or staff, only 18 percent of medical schools provide child care, only 14 percent of residency programs offer part-time or shared residency positions, and only 5.5 percent of medical schools have job-sharing.[23]

As you make your way through medical training and enter the work force, it is paramount that you learn the policies of every institution and organization with which you become affiliated regarding: family leave policies, work schedules, child care facilities, and tenure track timetables.

An important issue that is beginning to surface is the interruption of careers of women (and men). Family responsibilities, such as caring for children and aging parents, or moving with spouses, can and do interrupt a woman scientist's career with few opportunities for reentry. As a result, a disturbing number of women who are educated, who have made a commitment to medicine and science, are lost at a time when most men are moving into their most productive years.

In response to the public, scientific, and congressional concern about women's health and women's health research, in 1991 NIH established the Office of Research on Women's Health (ORWH) within the Office of the NIH director. The ORWH has initiated efforts to increase the number of women in biomedical careers and to facilitate their advancement. Central to this effort has been an attempt to identify barriers to the entry, advancement, promotion, and reentry of women into biomedical careers, including the practice of medicine and participation in biomedical and behavioral research.

MINORITIES AND RACIAL DISCRIMINATION

All the issues that apply to women in general have been said to be even more problematic for minority women. For many minority women, to be in a position where a "glass ceiling" comes into effect is an improvement. In fact, in the past many minority women believed that having a medical career especially in research, was not only unrealistic, but out of reach. In addition, minority women have often lacked minority role models. However, programs such as those sponsored by the National Medical Fellowships, Inc., to promote experiences in research and academic medicine for minorities, are helping to alleviate this.

Special attention to minority women in all programs is important, with identification of recruitment efforts for minority women into graduate medical and research programs, and increasing research initiatives aimed at minority women's health issues. Mentoring, and examples of minority women who have been successful in their careers in medicine, are vital to the continued encouragement and recruitment of minority women into medical careers.[24] The National Medical Association sponsors the National Minority Mentor Recruitment Network to identify factors that will increase the numbers of qualified African-Americans and minorities in the applicant pool and to provide mentors to serve as primary contact points for minority medical students making career choices during their professional training. The National Hispanic Mentor Recruitment Network, and other programs to increase the number of Hispanic women in medicine, are being sponsored by the Interamerican College of Physicians and Surgeons.

THE CHALLENGE IS CLEAR

While there continue to be barriers to the recruitment, retention, and advancement of women in medicine and other biomedical careers, the increased participation of women and the broader perception of the value of women's roles in medicine and science are providing increasing opportunities for women in the healing arts. Entering the field of medicine marks the beginning of a unique opportunity, with the ultimate ability to improve the status of health in our communities at large. Women have unique strengths, capabilities, and sensitivities that can enhance the ability of the health care system to provide gender-appropriate care. There are also diverse opportunities available for women to participate in not only primary care medicine as generalists, but also as specialists, investigators, educators, and administrators. The challenge is for each woman to utilize to the fullest her intellectual abilities and humanistic awareness, with perseverance and dedication.

REFERENCES

1. Women in Medicine Month. Women in Medicine Services. American Medical Association, Chicago, 1993.
2. White, P.E. *Women and Minorities in Science and Engineering: An Update.* National Science Foundation, Washington, 1992, Document No:NSF 92-303.
3. Bickel, J., Galbraith, A., and Quinnie, R. *Women in Academic Medicine: Statistics, July 1993.* Association of American Medical Colleges, Washington, D.C., 1994.
4. Section for Student Services Data Sheet, Association of American Medical Colleges, Washington, D.C. 1994.
5. *Minority Students in Medical Education: Facts and Figures VII.* L. Bergeisen, Ed. Association of American Medical Colleges, Washington, D.C. 1993.
6. Op. cit., Bickel.
7. Hirvela, E.R. "Surgery 2001; twilight of the gods." *Arch Surg* 1993; 128:658-662.
8. Organ, C.H. "Toward a more complete society." *Arch Surg* 1993; 128:617.
9. "Programs and Residents in Graduate Medical Education in 1991." *JAMA* 1992: 268, Appendix II, Table 1, in Women in Medicine Month, AMA.
10. Op. cit., Organ.
11. Op. cit., Programs and Residents.
12. Op. cit., Hirvela.
13. Kletke, P.R., Marder, W.D., and Silverger, A.B. "The growing proportion of female physicians: implications for the US physician supply." *AJPH* 1990; 80:300-304.
14. *Women in Medicine; Data Source.* Women in Medicine Services. American Medical Association, Chicago, 1993.
15. *U.S. Medical School Faculty 1993; Faculty Roster System.* Association of American Medical Colleges, Washington, 1993.
16. AAMC Women in Academic Medicine Statistics, July 1993.
17. Op. cit., Bickel.
18. National Institutes of Health, *Women in NIH Extramural Grant Programs: Fiscal Years 1981-1990*, Statistics, Analysis and Evaluation Section, Information Systems Branch (Bethesda, MD, 1991).

19. Summary, Public Hearing on Recruitment, Retention, Re-entry, and Advancement of Women in Biomedical Careers, in *Comprehensive Report of the Office of Research on Women's Health, Fiscal Years 1991-1992.* Department of Health and Human Services, National Institutes of Health, Public Health Service, Bethesda, Publication No. 93-3455.
20. Bernstein, A. E. and Donoghue, G.D. "Planning your academic promotion." *JAMWA* 1991; 46:87-90.
21. *National Institutes of Health: Women in Biomedical Careers, Strategies for the 21st Century.* U.S. Department of Health and Human Services, Public Health Service, in press.
22. Carr, R., Friedman, R.H., Moskowitz, M.A., Kazis, L.E., and Week, H.G. "Research, academic rank, and compensation of women and men faculty in academic general internal medicine." *J Gen Intern Med* 1992; 7:418-423.
23. Silva, B.M. "Pregnancy during residency: a look at the issues." *JAMWA* 1992; 47:71-74.
24. George, A.R. "African-American women in the medical profession." *JNMA* 1991; 83:954-957.

THE JOYS OF MEDICAL SCHOOL

PART 3

DOLLARS AND SENSE: FINANCING MEDICAL SCHOOL

Peter E. Lavine, M.D., and

Charles W. Carpenter

"The day which one starts out is

not the best time to start

one's preparations."

—Nigerian Proverb

CHAPTER 9

Paying for your medical school education is a serious and significant obligation. A variety of options need to be carefully considered because of the high cost of a medical education. In fact, given the current costs of attending a private medical school, a student who must rely totally on financial aid to pay for his or her tuition could likely take on an educational debt that exceeds $150,000. If attempts aren't made to control the amount of the loan, it could balloon to almost $800,000, or approximately $3,200 a month in student loan payments.

The basic philosophy of student financial assistance is that the ultimate responsibility of financing an education rests with you—the student—and your family. However, realizing that few students can pay for school outright, financial aid offices make every reasonable attempt to provide financial assistance. Every medical school participates in a variety of federal, state, institutional, and privately funded student financial assistance programs to help meet students' needs. Unfortunately, the majority of these programs are for educational loans; scholarship and grant monies are extremely limited for medical students.

There are repayment options that can help you manage a significant loan debt, such as deferment, forbearance, and consolidation—as well as loan repayment options with service commitment provisions. However, funding levels and eligibility qualifications for these options cannot be guaranteed for the future—and the loans must be repaid.

FINANCIAL PLANNING IS PARAMOUNT

We'd like to suggest a four-step process that will help you get control over your finances—before they control you. First, create an annual budget for each of the years you'll be in school, itemizing your expenses into five major categories: rent and utilities, food, transportation, medical, and personal. All fixed (tuition and fees) and directly related controllable costs (books and supplies) should be included in the budget plan as well.

Second, itemize all of your possible resources. This would include your income and any financial assistance you can get from family and friends, as well as loans at reasonable rates. Third, compare your budget with your resources to determine your unmet needs. And, finally, look for ways to cut costs and then compare your expenses and resources with the living-expense allowance of each prospective medical school's financial aid budget to help you determine the feasibility of attending it.

The discrepancy between expenses and resources available can be very intimidating. But don't panic! The vast majority of medical students cannot afford medical school. Let's briefly consider some available financing options.

EXAMINING YOUR OPTIONS

Generally state schools are significantly less expensive than private schools and easier to gain acceptance.

FINANCIAL OPTIONS

- Very rich uncle
- Armed Forces Health Professions Scholarship Program (APSP)
- Service Commitment Programs
  National Health Service Corps (NHSC)
  NHSC Loan Repayment Program
  State and private sponsored programs
- Loans and work-study
  Federal Stafford Loan (formerly Guaranteed Student
    Loan, GSL)
  Federal Unsubsidized Stafford Loan (formerly Supplemental
    Loans for Students, SLS)
  Federal Perkins Loan
  Health Education Assistance Loans (HEAL)
  Primary Care Loan (formerly HPSL)
  Medloans Alternative Loan Program (ALP)
  MedCap Medical Alternative Loan (MAL)
- Scholarships and grants
  Exceptional Financial Need (EFN)
  Financial Assistance for Disadvantaged Health

The Armed Forces have programs in which you receive a stipend for tuition and living expenses. In return, you owe the military service for each year that they have financed. This is an excellent option and often provides great experience. However, read the fine print! You may have to do a military residency rather than a civilian residency, and a military residency does not count as your payback time, although it does count toward military retirement benefits. The contract you sign will not be paid back for at least eight to ten years: after four years of medical school plus three to six years of residency. You must be sure you are willing to commit to four years of service following your entire training. The biggest benefit? No debt.

The federal government used to have a fairly well-developed Service Commitment Program, where the government (state or federal) pays for your school and living expenses. The payback is that you practice medicine in a rural area or an area designated as high need for medical services. Unfortunately, the program has dwindled into virtual oblivion. If the president and Congress are serious about providing increased health care, this is certainly a program to be expanded.

Another popular option is to "beg and borrow" loans. There are a variety of sources—federal, state, institutional, and private. Before you sign on this dotted line, you should try and understand the long-term costs of accrued interests. You'll want to try to pay off at least the interest to lessen the financial repayment hardships. Federal loan programs are described in Appendix B at the end of the book.

Generally, medical students do not have time for work-study jobs. But necessity may win out. There are some pearls, however. Evening desk or security jobs may allow you to study while at the same time earn some money. Libraries and apartment buildings are excellent examples. A number of medical students work as waiters or bartenders a couple of nights a week. Look for opportunities to do research or work in a clinic or office. If you are an early-riser, consider working on a blood-drawing team or history and physical team in a hospital.

Scholarships and grants are awarded on the basis of both financial need and academic standing. Most do not require repayment. Two examples are Exceptional Financial Need (EFN) and Financial Assistance for Disadvantaged Health (FADHPS). (See Appendix B.)

Another avenue for support is the service commitment opportunities with a hospital or doctor's practice. This type of arrangement provides the student with scholarship dollars in return for a service commitment.

MEETING YOUR FUTURE OBLIGATIONS

Given the likelihood that you will have to participate in some type of commercial, credit-based loans (e.g., HEAL, MAL, or ALP), we suggest that you obtain and examine a copy of your credit report prior to entry into a medical school. Early examination will let you detect and correct any errors and clear up negative items. Since correcting a credit report can be a time-consuming procedure, it is advisable to begin the process as soon as possible.

An increasing number of financial aid search services advertise their success at helping students obtain millions of dollars in "unclaimed" aid. Typically these services charge $50 or more. While some are reputable companies, please take care when contracting with them. You may find that you have paid for information easily obtained free through medical school financial aid offices. A good source of financial aid information is college scholarship source books, which are available in public and university libraries.

Careful planning and fiscal management is essential to meet your future obligations. You must think seriously about your capability to finance your education and to seek out good and reputable financial counseling and debt management services.

The cost of medical education can loom as a large financial hurdle. However, with plenty of hard work, motivation, early planning, and research that hurdle can be easily navigated and your goal of obtaining a medical education realized. The cost does not have to prevent the completion of a medical education or your choice of a medical specialty. There are opportunities and programs available to assist you. Don't forget your goal: to have a successful, busy practice and a fulfilling career.

PATIENCE AND PERSISTENCE: SURVIVING MEDICAL SCHOOL

Ruth Kevess-Cohen, M.D.

"All progress is precarious, and the solution of one problem brings us face-to-face with another problem."

—Reverend Martin Luther King, Jr.

CHAPTER 10

Once admitted to medical school, your chances of completing your four years successfully and qualifying to proceed to residency training are excellent. Since it is in the interest of both student and school, the typical medical school will provide special assistance to any student who needs it, in order to ensure that each student accepted can complete the degree program. However, the process of becoming a physician can be arduous and stressful, demanding more of one's inner resources and talents than most of us have needed to muster before. It is a process through which young men and women from disparate backgrounds and a wide variety of outlooks and attitudes are molded into professionals with a common ethos and a common language.

So how can you survive—and thrive—in medical school? The process starts early, with your decision to pursue a medical career. Taking the time to be sure this is what you really want to do—and not your parents' dream or the result of peer pressure—will pay off later, during late nights of studying and long shifts on call.

Another key survival factor is your choice of medical school. A highly competitive, grades-oriented school may not suit a student who performs best in a less pressured environment. If you enjoy close family ties you may do better in a medical school located near your family or friends. A newly married couple may benefit from choosing a medical school near the family of the nonmedical student. Of course, you may not have the luxury of choice, but when you do, taking such factors into account can make a big difference to the quality of your life during those four years.

When I was in my senior year in college, my fiancé was offered an attractive legal position in a firm located in Washington, D.C., his home-town. Suddenly, the array of medical schools to which I could apply was narrowed to the few located in the D.C./Baltimore area. My first choice of school was Johns Hopkins—the day I received my letter of acceptance was one of the happiest days of my life.

Determined to place as high a priority on the survival of our marriage as success on the job and in medical school, we decided that living halfway between the cities and commuting by car was out. We decided to split the commute evenly: we would live in D.C. for my first two years of medical school, when basic science classes met from 9 a.m. to 5 p.m. and there was no night call. I would take the train to Baltimore daily. The next two years we would live in Baltimore, and my husband would do the reverse commute daily. We decided against maintaining separate residences in the two cities, seeing each other only on weekends. We felt that such an arrangement would only increase the stress on our marriage, and we had seen the adverse effects on others who had attempted long-distance relationships. By placing a priority on seeing each other daily, we were making a statement that we would not allow our educational or career goals to sabotage the happiness in our personal lives.

STRATEGIES FOR THE FIRST TWO YEARS

Surviving medical school requires different skills and different approaches in the first two years compared to the second two years. Although many medical schools are now incorporating clinical training into the first and second years, the first two years usually comprise training in history-taking and physical exams, and observing and assisting working primary care doctors in their offices. But the main focus is on the basic medical sciences. Intensive course work in anatomy, biochemistry, physiology, pharmacology, pathophysiology, pathology, and others usually entails up to eight hours of lectures, discussions, and laboratory work daily. Careful note-taking is a must, and sleeping in class won't do! After a hurried dinner, most students spend several hours studying in their rooms or in the library; frequent exams demand many late nights of studying. The sheer volume of facts and concepts to be learned and memorized can be daunting.

Many medical students are used to receiving high grades in college with only moderate effort. In medical school, the same level of achievement can require a much more intensive effort. Yet, first- and second-year grades in medical school are almost never as important as grades were in college, during the years spent in preparation for medical school acceptance. Remember—you've gotten in! Now the important thing is to concentrate on learning as much as you can, in order to absorb the wealth of knowledge in basic medical sciences that will be the foundation for your clinical skills in the second two years.

Although there is no escaping the importance of logging those hours studying, there are ways to lessen the burden:

- Pick the right place to live and study. Do you enjoy studying with others or are you most comfortable on your own? If you become anxious seeing others cramming around you, don't room with other medical students, or at least pick a roommate in a different year of medical school.

- Be sure you have a comfortable, quiet place to study. This may mean negotiating with roommates, a spouse, or a significant other for space and time to get your work done.

- Be disciplined about keeping up. Don't skip classes or leave studying to the last few hours before an exam. You won't learn the material and the whole experience will be less satisfying. It helps to build study time into each day. For example, I spent the hour-long train ride to Baltimore each morning and evening reviewing class notes, reading textbooks, and studying for exams.

- Establish friendships for moral support. They will see you through these tough years and may last a lifetime. Attend social functions, eat meals together, study together, help each other. A concept which may be crystal-clear to you may be confusing to another. Remember, the cutthroat years are behind you. You are in this together; by helping each other, you all may benefit.

- Join a note-taking cooperative. Many medical school professors emphasize study from detailed class notes. If permitted by the professor, each class hour a different student can take extra-detailed notes and provide photocopies to the rest of the class. Although you should still attend class and take your own notes, these extra notes can provide back-up information you might otherwise miss.

- Learn to tolerate "difficult" professors. Though a given teacher may seem unfair or arbitrary at times, or material may appear on an exam that you believe was not taught, try to remain calm and reasonable. Compare notes with classmates. If the sentiment is widespread, a small group of students could approach the teacher politely to convey the class' concerns. If the matter is serious and the teacher does not respond, you may need to contact someone higher up in the administration, usually the dean of students.

- Don't let problems mount. If you are falling behind, failing your studies, or disturbed by personal problems, such as marital discord, illness, or substance abuse, go for help early, visiting student health services or talking with the dean/assistant dean of students. These are people who have been chosen for their abilities to relate well to students and have been trained to help you cope with and overcome your difficulty. Remedies include tutoring, personalized counseling, rehabilitation programs, and a leave of absence. In each case you can be assured that your concerns will be taken seriously and will be kept confidential. Many medical students feel that to become a good doctor they must appear invincible, so they are reluctant to admit to any weaknesses. But problems not addressed in the preclinical years are likely to worsen later, when longer hours and sleepless nights further tax one's relationships and coping skills.

■ Try to maintain nonmedical-related interests and activities. This will help you keep a more balanced perspective on your studies. One classmate of mine played the flute regularly in ensembles during medical school; another crocheted afghans for friends and relatives; others became involved in their churches or other community activities.

In late spring, after your second year, you will have to prepare for the U.S. Medical Licensing Examination (USMLE). It was established by the Federation of State Medical Boards of the U.S. Inc., and the National Board of Medical Examiners to provide a common evaluation for all medical licensure applicants. The exam is given in three steps. Step 1 assesses basic biomedical science, Step 2, clinical science, and Step 3, both biomedical and clinical science knowledge and application in patient management. Some medical schools require passage of Step 1 before promotion to clinical year and Step 2 prior to graduation. Step 3 is administered by each state medical licensing authority. Each jurisdiction has its own eligibility requirements. For more information on the USMLE you can contact: USMLE Secretariat, 3750 Market Street, Philadelphia, PA 19104-3290, (215) 590-9600, for their information bulletin. This exam is not to be taken lightly. It has delayed/killed many medical careers in the making.

THE CLINICAL YEARS

During the clinical years, years three and four, you will be developing the intellectual and hands-on skills necessary to care for real patients. You will learn to examine patients who are uncooperative, uncomfortable, or in pain; to draw blood and insert intravenous lines; to perform some laboratory tests, such as urinalyses and Gram stains; and do detailed write-ups of patient cases. Though the learning process can be fraught with anxiety, it is also tremendously rewarding. After all, now you are truly on your way to becoming a "real" doctor.

Clinical rotations usually last for one month at a time, although they can vary in length from two weeks to two months. The basic rotations, such as Internal Medicine, Family Practice, Surgery, and Pediatrics, usually are taken during the third year, with elective work in medical subspecialties or fields such as Radiology and Ophthalmology in the fourth year. On a typical rotation, you will be assigned, along with one or two other medical students, to a clinical team consisting of one or two residents, two or three interns, and supervising or attending doctors.

You will be an integral member of the team, attending all work rounds and teaching sessions, and will be "on-call"—usually sleeping over in the hospital every third or fourth night with other members of the team. You will be supervised at all times and will not be expected to make diagnostic or treatment decisions on your own.

Surviving the third and fourth years depends on patience and persistence: patience with yourself, when it seems like there is so much more to learn and you feel like you don't know anything yet, and persistence in pursuing all the learning opportunities available. Humility is an asset. You are expected to admit what you don't know and ask plenty of questions. Acting cocky or overconfident will get you in trouble with patients and supervising doctors alike. Be organized— you're expected to learn how to keep track of lots of pieces of data, from lab test results to daily urine outputs. Being compulsive about having all these facts at your fingertips will earn you lots of points. It also helps to make the time to read about your patient's medical conditions: You may find you can contribute uniquely to your patient's care, which will boost your confidence while impressing other team members.

During the third year, you'll begin thinking about the field in which you will do your residency, though a decision is not needed until the fourth year. Certain specialties require specific rotations to be taken prior to applying, so that recommendations are available from professors in the field of your choice. Careful planing can mean the difference between an acceptable residency match and a great one.

So, remember: be optimistic, be patient, and plan carefully. When those first four years of training are finally over, you'll be a better person just knowing what you've accomplished and that you survived. Better still is knowing that these basic survival principles will wind up being your "best friends" for many more years to come!

MATCH DAY AND MORE: CHOOSING A RESIDENCY

Peter E. Lavine, M.D.

"Quick decisions are unsafe decisions."

—Sophocles

Medical education in the United States occurs in three major phases. The first phase, which is medical school, is considered "undergraduate medical education." The second phase, "graduate medical education," prepares the physician for practice in a medical specialty and involves a training period referred to as a "residency program." Also considered a part of the graduate medical education process is a "fellowship," a more advanced training program. The third phase is a type of postgraduate medical education known as "continuing medical education." It involves a lifelong commitment to learning and is an essential feature of all medical professions.

It is during phase two, the residency program, where you begin to concentrate on a specific area of medicine (see box below). The residency provides you with the educational foundation and exposure to the area of medicine you want to pursue as a career. As a resident, you will find yourself assuming progressively greater responsibility for patient care. And it is during this period that you will begin to understand and comprehend the complexities and intricacies that are involved with patient care. Four years of medical school gives you the title "Medical Doctor," but not the experience required to actually practice medicine.

Areas of Medicine in Established Residency Programs

Allergy and Immunology	Ophthalmology
Anesthesiology	Orthopedic Surgery
Colon and Rectal Surgery	Otolaryngology
Dermatology	Pathology
Diagnostic Radiology	Pediatrics
Emergency Medicine	Physical Medicine and
Family Practice	Rehabilitation
Internal Medicine	Preventive Medicine
Medical Genetics	Psychiatry
Neurology	Radiation Oncology
Neurosurgery	Surgery
Nuclear Medicine	Thoracic Surgery
Obstetrics/Gynecology	Urology

The number of years of residency training varies. Internal medicine is generally a three-year residency, as is pediatrics. Other residencies, such as OBGYN, require four years of training; orthopedic surgery and general surgery require five years; and neurosurgery requires seven years of training. In a broad sense, the year of internship is simply the first year of residency. Some residencies allow you to do different types of internships, for instance, a general internship, surgical internship, medical internship, or transitional internship. You will receive financial support from your place of residency, and will be provided with professional liability coverage for the duration of your medical education.

Each residency program must meet specific requirements as determined by the Accreditation Council for Graduate Medical Education (ACGME). The ACGME comprises representatives from the American Board of Medical Specialties, the American Hospital Association, the American Medical Association, the Association of American Medical Colleges, the Council of American Specialty Societies, and a nonvoting member appointed by the Secretary of the U.S. Department of Health and Human Services. An annual in-depth description of all of the requirements for graduate medical education is available in the *Graduate Medical Education Directory*; referred to as the "Green Book." This essential resource is available in any medical school library.

DECIDING ON THE RESIDENCY PROGRAM

In general, medical students are asked to decide on a residency when they really are ill-equipped to do so. Due to the structure of the present system, you often have to start considering which residency to choose in the beginning of the third year of medical school, and have to make a final decision by the beginning of your fourth year—prior to completing a medical school rotation on each service. This is unfortunate because the bulk of the clinical exposure to the different residency programs occurs during the third and fourth year of medical school. A better system would have you do a general medical internship, during which you would apply to residency programs. This way you would have completed all of your medical school rotations and had sufficient exposure to a variety of specialties. Choosing early makes the decision harder—but you won't be alone.

Many medical students allow external factors to influence their decision, for instance, length of the residency, prestige of the residency, lifestyle of the residency, relative financial gains of one residency over another, and the difficulty of a residency. Try not to let these factors influence your choice of residency—and don't equate the lifestyle of the residency with the lifestyle of a real-life private practice. They aren't the same. When you complete your residency you can pick and choose from a variety of practice parameters and so tailor your practice toward the lifestyle you prefer.

The single-most important factor in choosing a residency is determining the area of medicine that excites you intellectually. If you follow this simple suggestion, you will be content with your work, be good at what you do, and become well-respected in your field.

APPLYING FOR RESIDENCY

With your choice of residency made, you begin the stressful process of obtaining it. Before you do anything else, request applications for each residency program you plan to apply to. It often takes a month or longer to receive the applications, and it takes time to accurately complete them. By obtaining the documents early and developing a good curriculum vitae, you can avoid the panicked rush that occurs as deadlines approach. As with any application process, the earlier you apply the better.

A good way to enhance your chance of obtaining the residency position you want is to do a rotation at the hospital in which you are interested, and let the decision makers meet you and evaluate your performance. If you are applying for an extremely difficult and competitive residency, you must be realistic about your chances for acceptance and formulate a backup plan. For example, if you apply to very competitive OBGYN programs, consider applying to a couple of transitional internships, or other less competitive programs, to ensure that your medical training continues. You can always re-apply to a residency program. In fact, a strong internship year will often improve your chances of getting into a residency program which was denied on the initial attempt.

Many students become torn between two residency choices, for example, otolaryngology and urology. If you find yourself in this situation, I recommend that you request applications for both specialties early. Then, when you decide which area is of most interest, you won't be late in the application process. Your final choice must, however, be made prior to "Match Day."

MATCH DAY

The match is one of the most memorable and legendary days of medical school. It evokes fear, anxiety, anger, elation, and relief. The National Residency Matching Program is a computerized system by which the medical student and the residency are matched together, creating a binding contract for the upcoming year. The concept of the match was developed to protect both student and institution from clandestine, behind-the-scenes handshakes that result in residency contracts and disgruntled employers or employees.

While the exact dates vary year to year, generally by January 15 all medical students are required to list, in order of preference, all of the residency programs to which they are applying. At the same time, the residency program directors are required to submit, in order of preference, all of the applicants being considered for their residency programs. A computer matches the top choice of the residencies with the top choice of the residency applicants.

These data are kept secret until a day in mid-March, called "Match Day," when all medical students throughout the nation are assembled at their medical schools and envelopes are distributed containing the results. Most applicants obtain the residency they seek, but a certain number of medical students will not match with any residency program, and a certain number of residency programs will not match with any applicants. However, by the end of the next day, most if not all, applicants will have a residency position and most residency positions will be filled.

For specifics on who participates in Match Day, refer to the "Green Book." Special requirements exist for foreign-born medical graduates of U.S. and non-U.S. medical schools, American graduates of foreign medical schools, and Armed Services residency applicants.

You can always change or switch residencies if you find you have made the wrong choice. Try to avoid the mind-set that you have wasted time in the "wrong field." The most important objective is to choose a field that you can enjoy. Once you have made your decision, work hard, apply early, and be yourself. Unless you consciously resist the pull, you will gravitate toward the field that complements your personality. Don't be intimidated by "horror stories" and uninviting statistics. When choosing your residency, follow your instincts and passion.

MED SCHOOL AT 37: LIFE AS AN OLDER MEDICAL STUDENT

Lawrence S. McDonald, M.D.

"They are able because they think they are able."

—Vergil

Age is relative. If Methuselah really lived 900 years, when he turned 37 he would have been considered an infant! However, when you are 37 and just beginning medical school, you definitely fall into the category "old." When I applied to medical school, I was informed that my age was at least a handicap. I had to offer a very good explanation of why I should take a seat in medical school, when I was 15 years older than the average student applying for that position.

The logic behind the demand was very simple—it costs hundreds of thousands of dollars to train a physician above and beyond the actual tuition. The value expected in return for this financial commitment is years of service to the patient population, the community, and the profession. My job was essentially to convince the admission officer that how I had spent the last 15 years would enhance my medical education, rather than detract from it.

I certainly had experienced the American dream—a lovely home, a lovely wife, and three kids in private school. I held a well-respected position in the para-medical community, and had donated a good number of hours to public service. Why did I want to give this up to go back to school and start all over again?

STARTING ALL OVER AGAIN

When one makes a decision to do something and feels that it is the best decision, whatever obstacles present themselves can be overcome. I had to face people telling me that getting into medical school would be difficult—some said that it would be impossible, most were sure it would never happen. Still, I did have a group of supporters who thought it was a wonderful idea. Of course wanting something and feeling it's the right thing does not necessarily make it happen, particularly in medical education.

Whether and where you go to school is in the hands of a number of people who don't know you at all. Even under the best set of circumstances, when people review your grades, your MCAT scores, your supporting data, and your recommendations, a lot of best guessing occurs.

I applied to a number of schools and was finally accepted at the Medical College of Pennsylvania. One of the more interesting things that the dean said to me was, "Be careful, you might really get what you wish for." I feel it was her way of warning me that everything that looks glorious and seems right can be very difficult and demanding, and that wishes can incur debts that we must pay.

I embraced school with vigor, but it was a difficult experience. I believe that medical educators are correct in saying that the older you are the more difficult it is to learn the material. But once having learned something, it does stay with you better.

WITH AGE COMES EXPERIENCE

The basic science part of medical school saw no advantages for me in being older. However, when I moved to the floor and did rounds in the clinical years, I found that the patients would often turn to me for answers to their questions, because I obviously was the more mature student. This made for some awkward moments, but it also gave me the opportunity to relate to patients at an early stage of my education. Fortunately, the team of people I worked with were more than happy to bail me out if I found myself in over my head.

In fact, I think the most advantageous aspect of being the older student was my ability to relate to the patients, particularly patients who also were older. I think the elderly felt more comfortable talking to someone who they knew was not a "teenager." This acceptance helped me become a better doctor by heightening my awareness that when people are acutely ill they not only need answers to their questions, but time to talk about their diseases and their options for treatment.

While patients seemingly deferred to me because of my age, that was not true of my classmates. They viewed me as just another student, because we all had the same responsibilities—and burdens. One of the more difficult aspects of medical training—not just medical school, but the internship and residency—is that there is very little time left to build relationships or to nurture already existing ones. And so, a good deal of emotional nourishment comes from your classmates. I always found it fascinating that someone would call at 1:00 in the morning and say "Lets go play racquetball for an hour." If that's the only time you can exercise and release your frustrations, then it's exactly the appropriate time. And so, there I would be at 1:00 a.m., joining my classmates for a serious game of racquetball.

Age may be an obstacle to admission to medical school, but it is not an obstacle to performance. While I don't plan on living 900 years, each day I expect wonderful things to happen. And for the most part, I am never disappointed.

TRAINING AND CREDENTIALING

TRAINING, TRAINING . . . AND MORE TRAINING: INTERNSHIP/ RESIDENCY/ FELLOWSHIP

Catherine L. Salem, M.D.

"If you have knowledge, let others light their candles at it."

—Margaret Fuller

That's right . . . medical school is not enough. Your training continues with internship, residency, and perhaps a fellowship. It is all determined by the kind of doctor you want to be—and the specialty you decide to pursue. Making the right choice means everything about your future job satisfaction. It truly deserves some serious thought.

There are a number of factors to consider, which need to be weighed against what you think you'd like to spend the rest of your life doing. These include:

- how saturated and competitive the specialty is
- the type of patients (and families) you will be dealing with
- the type of doctors you'll be working with
- how sick patients will be
- the amount of time you will actually spend with patients
- the number of hours you will be working
- the setting in which you will be practicing (hospital or private office, small town or big city)
- the ease with which you will be able to make a geographic move if necessary

Since life during training is usually quite different from life afterward, you might want to consider talking with working doctors to get a feel for what you can expect when you start practicing.

It's safe to say that no matter what your choice, your first year after medical school will be a year in hell. It's known as internship. Just how many years of residency follow this internship is based upon your specialty choice, and the whims and wisdom of your specialty's Board of Whateverology. For example, to become a family practitioner, pediatrician, or internal medicine doctor, you'll spend three years in training. To become a surgeon, gynecologist, or radiation oncologist, you'll spend four to five years in training. If your choice of career leads you toward one of the medical or surgical subspecialties—training continues after residency. You'll go on to do a fellowship. (Don't worry, senior citizens are allowed!) Fellowships are usually one to three years in duration.

INTERNSHIP: ONE YEAR IN HELL

Well, now that we have a basic understanding of the process, let's get into daily life. Internship is one of the most grueling years of the entire training process. This is the year of transition from little or no responsibility to what seems like a boatload. Fortunately, you will have several senior residents watching over you, and attending doctors will be supervising your supervisors. The internship year is spent rotating through the various aspects of your future job. For instance, in a family practice internship you will be spending time in the intensive care unit, coronary care unit, pediatrics, labor and delivery, and the emergency room. Most specialties require a smorgasboard-like year so that you can learn the various roles of multiple specialists. It brings you an appreciation not only of *your* job, but your colleagues' as well, so you'll know when to call on them for help with a patient.

It's the long hours that really make internship so difficult. In years past, when interns didn't have as much to learn, newly graduated doctors spent only one year in training before hanging out a shingle. However, they actually lived in the hospital during that entire year—hence the name resident. While you won't be living in the hospital, it will certainly feel like it at times. Every third night will probably be spent in the hospital "on call." And called you will be, for every conceivable thing—from Mr. Smith's fever to Mrs. John's chest pain—for the big and the small, the urgent and the ridiculous, the interesting and the mundane. For all of it, you're on the front line. You are expected to know when it's time to call in a more senior resident to help out. And you will report on the night's activity to your supervisors in the morning; what you might like to conveniently leave out, the nurses will report.

Internship is a time to learn the art of efficiency, to learn to rely on those more experienced than you at all levels in the patient-care management team, to learn to relate well with your peers, and to interact well with your patients. This is not the time to expect to be treated like the captain of the ship. Not only will this lead to disaster in the realm of patient care, but it will gain you no respect from any of your colleagues. To clarify this, "those more experienced than you" include everyone in the hospital with a name tag, except the medical students.

THE MIDDLE YEARS: RESIDENCY

Internship does end relatively quickly, and soon you'll be moving on to slightly better hours. During the middle years of your training you will settle into a routine, supervising those below you and learning from those more advanced in their training. This portion of training varies greatly, depending on the specific field you have entered. The most difficult part of the middle years is becoming comfortable with added responsibility: You will find that important decisions rest more and more with you. During this time you will inevitably see some of your patients die. Not everyone is cured with an antibiotic and not everyone pulls through their medical emergencies, even with the best of care. Residency is a time of learning to give and to receive comfort as a caregiver.

The need for training after medical school also means that you have lots more learning ahead of you, and yes, a few more tests. The most important of these is the exam for Board Certification. This is the examination climax of your medical career—it certifies you as competent in your field of medicine. While residency is meant to prepare you for this exam, many of the long hours that you'll put in do not seem directly related. It will be your responsibility during residency to demand direction in your endeavor to become board certified.

During the final year of your residency training, you may have the opportunity and privilege to serve as chief or head resident: You will be in charge of a number of administrative tasks, like determining the call schedule or arranging for a lecture series to help prepare for board certification. If offered to you, take it—being head resident is a good experience and will be well thought of by those considering you for future endeavors. Future endeavors?!?! "You mean I'm not done yet?"

FELLOWSHIP COMES NEXT

If you have chosen a subspecialty, then the fellowship comes next. This can be quite an exciting time, for it lets you concentrate on what you really want to be doing. For example, the surgeon can now concentrate on just plastic surgery or cardiac surgery. The internal medicine doctor can spend time practicing only cardiology or gastroenterology. It may be clinically oriented, research-oriented, or a mix of the two. It lasts anywhere from one to three years, during which time you will be supervising residents in academic settings, and learning from peers. In general, you will spend fewer hours in the hospital and more hours reading.

The purpose of a fellowship program is to broaden your knowledge and experience in a narrow area within your given specialty and to expose you to a greater number of patients served by this area of medicine. It may be hospital- or university-based, which offers the advantage of a more academic setting. Or, it may place you with one or more doctors in private practice, which has the advantage of giving you first-hand patient experience. In many cases you are functioning just as you would if you were out in practice on your own. This is demonstrated by a new level of trust and responsibilities designated by your mentor or "teaching" physicians.

You will more than likely be studying for your specialty board exams during this time. Believe it or not, even at this point your education will not really be over, because as a physician you will be challenged by new techniques, ideas, and an ever-expanding pool of knowledge that will in most cases be matched by an insatiable desire to continue learning. Although it may seem like a great deal of work, it can be done. Perhaps most importantly, the fellowship years are a time to enjoy yourself, learn more about the nuances of medicine, fine-tune your technical skills, and take a good look at your bedside manner.

POST-GRADUATE ADVICE AND BEYOND

It seems as though the entire process of training to become a doctor is full of sacrifices. Right? Well, right and wrong. You are doing this because you want to be a doctor. In a way it is a selfish period of your life—after all, you are the one that is going to get the M.D. and specialty training. Please remember that all of the decisions you make should involve your family— whether that's your extended family, your spouse and/or children, your significant other, your parents and siblings, or your family of friends. Although you're the one who will be putting in lots of hard work, you will not be the only one who is sacrificing.

Medicine is an extremely time-consuming career, and to make matters worse, the times that you will be unavailable to your family are not always predictable. Inevitable stresses will be placed upon both your old and new relationships. These stresses are responsible for a high divorce and suicide rate among physicians. Being aware of the danger of ignoring these stresses is the first step toward preventative medicine for yourself and those you care about. Open, honest communication is a necessity. Forgetting about those around you will become a habit if allowed, and you will soon find yourself attaining personal educational goals but isolating yourself socially. The successful physician is not only an accomplished academician, but a well-rounded human being.

DECISIONS, DECISIONS: PRIMARY CARE VS. SPECIALTY CARE

Luette S. Semmes, M.D.

"The great aim of education is not knowledge but action."

—Herbert Spencer

An increasing number of medical specialties has developed over the years, and—not surprisingly—an increasing number of medical specialists. In fact, overall, more medical students are choosing to practice in a specialty rather than in primary care. What are the differences, and how do you decide between the two paths?

A LITTLE ABOUT EVERYTHING VERSUS EVERYTHING ABOUT A LITTLE

It is commonly said that the primary care physician needs to know a little about everything, while the specialist knows everything about very little. The idea of primary care is that doctors take care of the whole person, while doctors who have a specialty focus on the specific diseases of body systems. Your individual attitudes and aptitudes will determine which approach you chose. If you tend to see the big picture of things in life, if your idea about being a doctor is to be able to take care of almost any problem that your patient brings to you, then it sounds like you are cut out to be a primary caregiver. If you prefer to focus in on a problem, and are willing to assume responsibility for solving a problem others have been unable to solve, then becoming a specialist is most likely the best route for you to follow.

Ideally, the family doctor, whether an internist, family practitioner, or general practitioner, would be able to provide all care to his or her patients, treating the wide array of medical and surgical problems that arise. Each patient's medical history, social and family dynamics, medications, and idiosyncrasies would be well-known and efficiently managed by that one physician.

However, some specialty caregivers feel that they do provide primary care in their practice. For example, a diabetic may go to an internist or an endocrinologist for care of his diabetes. A patient with back pain may be cared for by an orthopedist, a neurologist, or even a phyciatrist. A number of factors, quite varied in nature, seem to be pushing medical students into choosing a specialty. Many feel there is too much to know. They are overwhelmed by the vast array of medical knowledge they need to have at their disposal to function as a competent primary care doctor. It is hard enough to remember everything that is learned in training. Add all the new information, procedures, and medications that are continually being introduced and the task becomes insurmountable.

A second reason for choosing a specialty has to do with human nature, and how one becomes more proficient at doing a job that is familiar. Would you rather have your cardiac catheterization done by someone who does the procedure every day or only a few times a year? Similarly, when there are thirty or more medications available to treat high blood pressure, the doctor who treats many patients with this problem will be better able to choose the most appropriate therapy. Closely tied to this is the fact that physicians, like professionals in any career, find there are certain aspects of their job that they enjoy and perform better than others. Good performance usually equals job satisfaction.

Finally, a third factor that I think makes primary care less attractive is the frequency of lawsuits in our society. The ease with which physicians are sued for mistakes that occur naturally encourages those in the medical field to practice a narrower and more manageable area of medicine.

The basic difference between these two types of practitioners is the depth of the relationship that develops between the patient and the doctor. Since the patient tends to be seen over time (sometimes a lifetime) by the family doctor with all of his or her illnesses or for preventive care, the doctor becomes more familiar with the patient as a whole—his or her attitudes toward care, psychosocial makeup, and previous experiences with ailments or medicines. This information can be as important to treating a patient effectively as making the correct diagnosis. But beyond this medical advantage is the deeper personal relationship that can develop between the caregiver and the patient. What the physician derives from the doctor-patient relationship may be one of his or her greatest rewards. But for others, personal and career satisfaction may come from other sources.

SOME PRACTICAL CONSIDERATIONS

The duration of training and earning potential is usually greater for someone who specializes than someone who practices primary care—

usually at least two years beyond the basic three- or four-year surgical, pediatric, or internal medicine residency. Some very specialized surgical fields require as many as seven years. As a result, the fees you receive for your training when in practice may differ two- to fourfold. One of the reasons for the difference in the training duration and pay scale revolves around the performance of procedures which are, for the most part, done more frequently by specialists—and the accompanying higher malpractice insurance. It is primarily the specialists who perform procedures, whether medical or surgical—and who command higher pay. Although there are movements afoot to decrease reimbursement for procedures and reward the practice of primary care, these differences will most likely persist in the near future.

In the end, I suggest you keep a few things in mind when considering your career choice. First, there is always flexibility within any field. Some primary care physicians become "specialists" in one aspect of medicine (e.g., adolescent medicine or nutrition). Over time, they may even forego traditional primary care medicine to concentrate on their field of interest. Similarly, some physicians who are trained in a specialty field may practice in a manner that is more reminiscent of a family doctor, either because they actually treat primary care problems or because their approach to their patients is more holistic. Second, when contemplating your choice familiarize yourself with the common, daily tasks that are a part of the job and ask yourself whether doing them day in and day out will engage you and keep you happy. It may be fun and challenging to repair the weekend athlete's ruptured tendon, but you may find that you cannot stand evaluating lowback pain ten times each day.

ESTABLISH YOUR CREDENTIALS: BECOMING BOARD-CERTIFIED

Renee R. Jenkins, M.D.

"If you have built dreams in the air, your work need not be lost; that is where they should be. Now put foundations under them."

—Henry D. Thoreau

Yes, you can practice medicine and in all likelihood lead a good life without taking a medical specialty certification exam. So, why would you want to put yourself through the painful process of preparing for yet another exam, let alone the additional loan you might have to take to pay for it (exams cost well over $1,000 in most cases)? The simple answer is: peer pressure! While there are little data that compare differences in earning power, there are data that show that significant differences exist in the percentage of doctors who are certified based on age, gender, location of training program, location and type of practice, and type of specialty. Other institutional issues will also vary in importance based on surrounding circumstances of location and type of practice. But at least you should have a better idea of what you're letting yourself in for, so here goes...

TAKING YOUR PLACE IN HISTORY

Physicians began to define themselves as specialists as early as the late 1800s and early 1900s by organizing themselves into specialty societies and colleges based on similar professional interests. These organizations served educational, social, and professional functions for their members and were usually based on a self-defined interest and approval from their peers. At first, membership was assumed to be indicative of some special competence, and so no formal examination existed. Soon, however, members came to believe that standards of excellence should be established and moved to define competence in their areas of specialty through a certification process. The first nationally recognized medical specialty board was founded for ophthalmology in 1917. Today, 23 boards and 24 specialties are recognized by the American Board of Medical Subspecialties and the AMA Council on Medical Education, not counting subspecialty certifications. In 1982, two out of three physicians who had five or more years of post-residency training were board-certified; by 1990, three out of four or approximately 276,000 post-residency physicians were certified. How will the emphasis on primary care in the age of healthcare reform impact on that trend? Stay tuned!

WHAT'S IN IT FOR YOU?

When you near the end of your residency training with license in hand, feeling the three to four years of post-call fatigue, and facing major medical school debt, you may find yourself wondering if medical specialty boards are worth the pain. Over 90 percent of pediatric cardiologists think so: They have the highest rate of board certification. Interestingly, only 15 percent of general practitioners think so: They're one of the lowest in percentage of board-certified practitioners. So, your decision will be based on a number of factors. Here's what I think you should consider.

Does the hospital where you plan to practice consider specialty boards in their credentialing process? Specialty boards in surgical specialty areas are more likely to be an issue than certification in Family Practice, Internal Medicine, or Pediatrics. Specialty certification for some board reviewers connotes competence based on the recognition of completion of an accredited residency program, examination by experts in the field, and meeting a certain national standard for a specialty area. However, there are those who believe that specialty certification should not be a requirement to participate in patient care. The Joint Commission on Accreditation of Healthcare Organizations, for example, believes that certification should be considered as one of the criteria, but clinical privileges should be based on training, experience, and demonstrated current competence. The problem is the criteria are a lot harder to measure—so many hospitals will opt for a measure that someone has already created.

The controversy has now moved out of the hospital and into managed care. Although the physician's personal attributes were rated almost as highly, certification or eligibility was the highest-ranked factor in recruiting and hiring physicians. This has created a very hot debate in areas with large numbers of men over 50, women, and international medical graduates who are more likely to be excluded from managed care systems. In some geographical areas this creates major access to care problems, but don't let me drift off to health care reform again, you get the picture!

Among the prizes for pulling yourself through the boards is membership in specialty societies, most of which require board certification for full membership. Why is it so important to be a part of those "clubs?" For those in academic settings, it's obvious—promotion and tenure. For those in practice—marketability. When you're certified, you immediately become recognized as one of the best in your particular area of specialization. Of course, excellent reputations exist for nonboarded specialists, but only after long periods of practice and proof of expertise through patient outcomes.

Most specialty programs, especially those in academic centers, press very hard for their residents to become board-certified since the accreditation process considers that a criterion of a good residency program. Is certification necessarily a measure of competence? This question is very controversial. In a study conducted by the American Board of Internal Medicine, noncertified internists scored lower on a written exam, rated lower in the eyes of peers related to clinical skills, and were less likely to conform to the preventive care standards. But compared to certified internists, their patient care outcomes were not significantly different for patients with chronic illnesses.

GET READY, GET SET, GO!

You've weighed your choices, your program director pressed you to the wall, your fellow residents have made it known that anyone who doesn't take the boards is a "chicken," so now what? First, find out the eligibility requirements for the board you wish to take. Usually the program director will have this information available, but you might also want to contact the board directly. The American Board of Medical Specialties has contact information on the individual specialty board members. Most boards also have information on the question format and review recommendations specific to that board, so it's certainly worth the effort to contact them. Candidates who have switched residencies or taken time off during residency training may need an individualized review of their records to be sure that time-criteria have been met. You also need to reconfirm the accreditation status of your residency program; these recommendations become part of your record and are often the basis upon which the program director approves your eligibility to sit for the examination. You may also review your performance on in-service exams if they are available and get specific tips on how to prepare yourself from the program director, who has probably guided a number of residents through this process and has some significant observations.

As with any examination application process be sure to get it in on time! The usual cost is in the range of $1,000, for the written examination—for those boards with oral examinations, there is an additional cost. Review courses are available for most boards, as well as review booklets to organize and sharpen your test-taking skills. Keeping up with reading and answering the questions on the board examinations are two different types of activities, and although one improves the other, nothing beats practicing for increasing a particular skill. The test formats are changing to a problem-solving mode rather than the regurgitation of facts, which is likely to be a better measure of clinical competence. Everyone predicts computer-based testing by the year 2000, so, even though you may miss it at the time of your initial board, you're very likely to get it at the time of recertification.

Oral examinations are so incredibly variable, your best information comes from the individual board and people who have taken it and passed. Eligibility requirements for the oral examination are often a certain number of years in practice and demonstration of a certain type of caseload—find out early.

The dreaded day comes! You take the exam, you feel not bad about it, you wait months for your score and wow—you missed passing by six points. Don't despair—no board has a 100 percent pass rate, and as I already told you—a board exam is not a direct measure of one's competence: it's a related, but not a direct measure. Review your difficult areas, reexamine your preparation strategy, talk with colleagues who passed the exam for suggestions, and get ready to take it again.

Next scenario: you pass. Can you put away those books, questions, crying towel, and memories of sleepless nights? No. Most boards are time-limited and have a recertification requirement. Again, there is terrific variability: some require a written recertification process similar to the initial board, others allow a take-home computerized exam. This should all be in the literature the board sent you.

My basic recommendations are, consider how important being certified is to your future, and if you decide it is, do it early. Don't put it off until you've been out of residency training a long time: The longer you've been out, the harder it is to prepare yourself. Get the information on your specialty board eligibility requirements and certification process from a reliable source. Plan your strategy to increase your likelihood of passing. If you don't pass, do it again until you do. Good luck!

BIBLIOGRAPHY

Budde, N.W., "Who are the non-certified physicians? What do we know about them?" in Langsley, D.G., Dockery, J.L., and Weary, P., *Health Policy Issues Affecting Graduate Medical Education*, American Board of Medical Specialties, Evanston, Illinois, 1992.

Goldstein, J.C., "Tracing the rise of specialty medicine," in Langsley, D.G., Dockery, J.L., and Weary, P., *Health Policy Issues Affecting Graduate Medical Education*, American Board of Medical Specialties, Evanston, Illinois, 1992.

Jacobs, M.O. and Mott, P.D., "Physician characteristics and training emphasis considered desirable by leaders of HMOs," *Journal of Medical Education*, 62: 725-731, 1987.

Langsley, D.G., "The use of specialty and subspeciality credentials for hospital privileges," in Langsley, D.G., and Stubblefield, B., *Hospital Privileges and Specialty Medicine*, 2nd Ed., American Board of Medical Specialties and American Hospital Association, Evanston, Illinois, 1992.

Mueller, C. Barber, "Implications for Licensure and Certification," in Neufield, V and Norman, GR (ED), *Assessing Clinical Competence*, Springer Series on Medical Education, Volume 7, 1985.

Ramsey, P.G., "Performance of non-certified specialists," in Langsley, D.G., Dockery, J.L., and Weary, P., *Health Policy Issues Affecting Graduate Medical Education*, American Board of Medical Specialties, Evanston, Illinois, 1992.

Wallace, A.P., "HMOs and physicians without board certification," *NEJM*, 328(20):1501-2, 1993.

STYLES OF

PRACTICE

M.D. OR MBA: MEDICINE IS A BUSINESS

Peter E. Lavine, M.D.

"Being in your own business is working 80 hours a week so that you can avoid working 40 hours a week for someone else."

—Ramona E.F. Arnett

Most physicians appreciate and understand that the practice of medicine is not only a science but an art. However, the business side of medicine as an aspect of private practice is ignored during the years of educational training. Therefore, many physicians, upon completing their medical training, suddenly find themselves running a small business for which they are totally unprepared. This often results in costly and inefficient mistakes at a time when they can least afford to make them. Because of the tremendous expense involved in opening a private practice, most young physicians are joining already established groups or HMOs in order to offset the financial burden.

As with any small business, planning is the key to success. Writing a business plan will help you set long- and short-term goals. The plan should cover issues such as: sources of financing, financial projections, a marketing plan, site/location evaluation, physician recruitment, equipment leasing, and the day-to-day mechanics of providing patient care.

Sound financial management is essential to the well-being of any small business. This involves developing a recordkeeping system detailing the income and expenses of your practice, employee salaries, business and professional insurance, rent and utilities, retirement plans, office and professional supplies, patient fees and payments, depreciation on equipment, consultant fees for attorneys and accountants, convention and meeting allocations, and so on. As with other small businesses, you are required by law to keep records that will enable you to complete an accurate income tax return. It would be a good idea to retain an accountant, attorney, and financial advisor.

STRUCTURING YOUR PRACTICE

There are many ways to structure your practice, for example: operating as a solo practitioner, sharing space with other physicians, forming a partnership, or forming a professional corporation with other physicians. Two or three physicians can join together and rent office space and share office personnel. This arrangement will keep costs to each physician low, while at the same time allowing each to practice independently. Incorporating is, of course, a much more formal relationship, where a separate legal entity is created. Since each option has its own legal, business, and tax advantages and disadvantages, you will want to consult with your lawyer and accountant.

You are also required to obtain certain insurance protections such as professional liability insurance against malpractice claims, insurance protection against workmen's compensation for any injuries that occur in the office, as well as flood and fire damage. Additionally, all Occupational Safety and Health (OSHA) regulations must be strictly adhered to.

OFFICE PLANNING CONSIDERATIONS

Renting office space that provides a sufficient amount of room for personnel, examination rooms, and equipment is crucial. The office layout is also extremely important in maintaining a peaceful and relaxed patient flow. Since rent is a major expense, office size should be determined by anticipated volume of patients. Handicap accessibility—now a legal requirement for any business—is vital for such practices as orthopedics, physical medicine and rehabilitation, and rheumatology. Available parking and public transportation are additional considerations when choosing office space.

HIRING AND RETAINING PERSONNEL

One of the best ways to determine your personnel needs is to develop an office procedure manual that will outline step-by-step guidelines for completing each office task, and provide clearly defined job descriptions with salary scales. Most medical offices have an office manager who supervises the office personnel and is responsible for overseeing the accounting and financial procedures of the office. It is imperative that the office manager provide you with accurate and timely financial data.

Additional office personnel might include:

- office receptionist, who is responsible for receiving patients, managing the phones, appointments, and daily bookkeeping tasks

- clinical assistant or nurse, who assists the physician with patient examinations and treatment, and is also responsible for patient history, routine lab procedures, collection and preparation of specimens, and other patient care concerns

■ insurance secretary, who files the claims and reports necessary to collect third-party fees, and handles questions and inquiries about billing claims

■ transcriptionist, who keeps accurate documentation of the patient evaluation

Employee salaries and benefits are a major component of your small business's overhead. To control the overhead and keep staffing to a minimum, you may want to use an outside agency for billing, payroll, and transcriptions. Or, you could use part-time employees to provide these functions.

SETTING UP SYSTEMS

As is true of most small businesses, a computer system is an indispensable tool for the billing, collecting, and insurance processing procedures, as well as for accounting, appointment scheduling, practice management, and transcription activities. The actual computer system you choose is best determined by consulting with your financial advisor, accountant, and a computer analyst. Prices vary and the configuration you choose will depend on the size and volume of your practice.

The telephone system is also a vital component to both the clinical and business aspects of your practice. Choosing the appropriate equipment involves a process of evaluation and comparative shopping. Since the telephone is likely to be the first point of contact with patients, it is important for your staff to be trained in its proper use. In addition, most physician offices use answering services, either live or electronic, to handle calls when the office is closed.

MARKETING YOUR PRACTICE

The idea of marketing your practice may make you feel uncomfortable. In fact, many physicians find the concept of advertising particularly distasteful. However, marketing can be viewed from another perspective: as an ongoing process that ascertains patients' needs and matches your services to those needs. Marketing can include direct attempts to reach patients as well as the establishment of a large network of referrals. For example, by becoming active in your community, you could meet a lot of potential patients. If you are active in the local medical society, you might meet physicians who could potentially refer patients to you.

Most physicians wish that they could simply practice medicine and ignore the small business aspects of their practice. This is not realistic. It is becoming even more difficult as government regulations increase and more market power is given to third-party payors. Physicians are being forced into managed-care situations where corporate profits are determining the allocation of health care. As physicians face increasing costs and decreasing reimbursements, this widening gap makes the business of medicine significantly more difficult. More importantly, it could eliminate solo practitioners completely. It is critical that before opening your practice, you discuss these plans with colleagues and consultants. To ensure that you take all the steps necessary, I highly recommend attending special preparatory courses offered by the American Medical Association.

WHERE TO HANG THAT SHINGLE: CHOOSING A PRACTICE LOCATION

Duane J. Taylor, M.D. and
Ronald E. Tinsley, M.D.

"Destiny is not a matter of chance, it is a matter of choice; it is not a thing to be waited for, it is a thing to be achieved."

—William Jennings Bryan

CHAPTER 17

A̲mong the many exciting career decisions facing you as a doctor-to-be is where to "hang your shingle" when you complete your training. For some, the decision is easy. We know several colleagues who from the very onset of their training had the intention of returning to their respective hometowns to practice medicine. Many doctors find themselves practicing in or near to where they complete their residencies. Still others look for locations far different from what they have experienced. For instance, a doctor who has trained in an urban hospital may long for a rural community in which to practice. Whether you feel certain that you know exactly where you want to set up shop—or don't have a clue—there are a number of factors you should consider as you begin to practice medicine.

QUESTIONS AND ISSUES TO CONSIDER

At the top of the list of considerations should be your family. If you are married or have a significant other whom you plan to include in your future, you must involve them in the decision. Remember, they will endure and enjoy the various ups and downs involved in your career and so deserve input into a decision that determines where they will be living and working. Other concerns you should address include:

- demand for your specialty
- economic development within the area
- cost of living
- weather
- urban vs. suburban vs. rural setting
- geographic proximity to family (yours and your partner's)
- dynamics of the physician community
- availability of cultural and social events

In the process of choosing a location, you might want to consider using the services of a company that specializes in helping physicians find practice types and locations that fit their criteria. In addition to reviewing the demographics of a city you may be interested in, there are sources of information regarding trends in practice types in specific locations. Your local and national medical societies can be of assistance in identifying these companies.

DR. TAYLOR:

During medical school I was advised to do my residency in a location where I thought I would potentially settle down and live. It would give me an opportunity to establish some roots, give me a feel for the medical community, and help me establish contacts with potential referring physicians. A technique which I found useful was to make a two-column list with rank-ordered pros and cons of potential cities and communities where I thought I would like to practice and live. From year to year during my training I would reevaluate the list. Interestingly, the rankings changed as my personal and professional preferences changed.

I decided to do my general surgery internship in Houston and my residency in Los Angeles. At the time, both were areas I thought I might be interested in living and both had training programs that I desired. While in each city I made a concerted effort to get a feel for the practice environments, as well as the nonmedical aspects of the communities that would contribute to the quality of my life. In the midst of my residency, however, I obtained a fellowship position on the east coast in Washington, D.C. (a city I had lived in and loved for a year while in high school). And so, despite the new friends and colleagues I had developed, I moved to D.C. where I was fortunate enough to meet the woman who is now my wife, and find a practice type and location that I enjoy.

DR. TINSLEY:

Alaska! The very name stirs excitement in the minds of those who savor adventure. This "Great Land" encompasses extensive mountain ranges, immense glaciers and river valleys of unbelievable proportions. The great whales, bears, king salmon, and eagles attract hordes of tourists to our 49th state but . . . doctors?

Alaska might well be at the bottom of your list of states to practice medicine; but don't disregard it. One of our local plastic surgeons described to me his subzero January trip to Fairbanks when deciding where he would practice. It occurred after several discouraging lower "forty-eight" interviews. But his warm reception prompted him to phone his wife and say, "Pack your bags dear, we're moving to Fairbanks!" They and their now-grown children and son-in-law are still pleased with a decision that was made some 19 years ago.

Of course, location and climate are important issues when contemplating a practice site. For instance, not only is Alaska a gigantic piece of real estate, but it comes with a diverse climate. Winters are darker and colder in the interior—around Fairbanks—than anywhere in all of the United States. Summers are usually warm and sunny, with no darkness between mid-May and mid-August. Southeastern Alaska (the Panhandle region around Juneau) has much warmer winters and cooler summers, and considerably more precipitation.

You also have to determine if there is enough of a client population to support your economic requirements. Distances are another factor. If you settle far from family, will you be willing and able to accept long travel hours and big bucks for airfares to and from your parents or spouse's parents? Or to attend professional meetings?

Family life, social events, schools, and recreation are usually the major items left to ponder once business opportunities are assured. Once I established my practice and settled into a comfortable home, I found that family life could be superb in Alaska. Though there are fewer people in huge geographical settings, the social atmosphere is as friendly as any place I've been.

LOOKING FOR SHANGRI-LA TO PRACTICE IN

So remember it's never too early to start gathering information about potential practice locations. Whether it's in the country, by the ocean, in a busy urban center or even in the desert, the decision of where to practice can be an exciting one. Although any location you consider will have some drawbacks, the *right* location is the one that will complement your career in medicine and be fulfilling to you, your spouse (or significant other), and family.

HAVE STETHOSCOPE, WILL TRAVEL: MEDICINE AS A TRANSPORTABLE CAREER

Maria L. Chanco Turner, M.D.

"Even the woodpecker owes his success to the fact that he uses his head and keeps pecking away until he finishes the job he starts."

—Coleman Cox

CHAPTER 18

Medicine has a lot to offer: intellectual challenge, fiscal stability, and best of all, the opportunity to help others. No matter what the circumstances might be a physician's knowledge is infinitely transportable and can improve other people's lives. A physician's daily occupation, when properly carried out, benefits society in general and patients in particular. At this stage of my career, my greatest joy in being a physician is the ongoing intellectual stimulation and challenge posed by basic scientific discoveries and translating them into improved day-to-day care of patients.

Although the milieu in which American physicians practice has changed over the years, and is in the throes of major alterations right now, I maintain that the basics of the profession and its inherent sources of satisfaction have not changed. There are a variety of paths to career satisfaction and if one is flexible, the journey can be both fun and fulfilling.

It had always been my goal to go into academic medicine and teach dermatology. However, other priorities—choice of residence, marriage, and motherhood—temporarily assumed more importance. Early in my career, I had made a decision that I would only marry a physician—the assumption being that it would be easier for a fellow-physician to understand personal and career requirements as they arose. This pivotal decision worked out extremely well. I also decided to only work on a part-time basis after becoming a mother until my children were older.

PART-TIME AT AN HMO

Despite the low regard with which HMOs and their physicians were held in the mid-1960s (it is only somewhat more acceptable now), I decided to practice Dermatology at Group Health Association, which was a pioneer HMO in the country. There were distinct advantages to working at a staff-model HMO: colleagues to share interesting patients with; easy access to patients' primary physicians and their complete medical charts; and an administrator who managed the business—and the office; the luxury of not having to worry about patients' ability to pay for follow-up visits, medications, or procedures; and longitudinal follow-up of patients. Did I lack independence? In my twelve years at the HMO, I practiced medicine as I would have in any other setting. My patients' welfare dictated my medical decisions.

While at the HMO, I decided to stay active on the part-time teaching staff of George Washington University medical school. I also participated at the clinical grand rounds at the National Institutes of Health. There was hardly a day that I did not have a student, intern, or resident following me as I saw my patients. Having students around kept me validating and articulating the reasons for my diagnoses and treatment decisions; I think it made me a better physician.

The best part of this period of my career was that I was "having my cake and eating it too." Working part-time, about twenty-four hours a week, meant that there was time to bake cookies and chaperone school field trips. It was great to have the kids tumble into the back seat of the car and vie to tell me about the latest happenings at school. There was time to have dinner parties. There was even time to shop. I felt fulfilled! All aspects of my life were getting an equal share.

FULL-TIME AT THE MEDICAL SCHOOL

Eventually, a full-time faculty position opened up at George Washington University and I realized I was ready. The transition from the HMO to academia was relatively smooth, except for two aspects. As much as I loved one-on-one teaching, I found lecturing before two hundred medical students a great and difficult challenge. Also, it took a while for me to become comfortable with charging for my services. It upset me when patients complained about their bill—and when they failed to pay it. However, the patients were challenging, lecturing did become easier, and it was gratifying to nurture and train students and residents. Despite all the jokes about the wonderful hours that dermatologists keep, full-time work really meant more than forty-hour weeks at the office, plus homework. There was less time for unscheduled, nonprofessional pursuits. Life was hectic—but very interesting.

ANOTHER MOVE—TO THE NATIONAL INSTITUTES OF HEALTH

Having a father who was a medical school professor and a mother who was a general practitioner, it's no wonder that at age four I knew I was going to be a physician. When we temporarily moved to a small rural town in the Philippines during World War II, I saw my parents deliver babies, instruct the townspeople on hygiene, and render medical care in the most humble of conditions. No money was exchanged, but we did not lack for rice, chickens, and eggs. And now, years later, I am a clinical dermatologist working at the National Institutes of Health. Besides its basic science laboratories, the National Institutes of Health has a clinical center for clinicians to take care of patients, teach clinical fellows, and do research. I am in yet another medical environment where diagnostic and therapeutic puzzles abound. I am challenged daily to come up with solutions. The answers are not always there; the task is to keep trying.

My career and my personal life have thrived in different settings by making slight adjustments. I feel it's possible to have it all. Medicine has a bright future in this country or my husband and I would not have actively encouraged our daughter, who is now in her third year of medical school, to invest her life in it!

Doctors Working Together: The HMO Experience

James R. Hughes, M.D.

"The health of the people is really the foundation upon which all their happiness and all their powers as a state depend."

—Benjamin Disraeli

CHAPTER 19

Change. It's always with us.

My "ENT" professor once stated, "Mine was the most important specialty there was . . . until Fleming discovered that [expletive] mold!" It was 1958. His field, known in the 1930s as Eye, Ear, Nose, and Throat, had indeed been the commonest of all American medical specialties— until the discovery of penicillin. Within only twenty years, the mastoidectomies, the incisions and drainage of peritonsillar and retropharyngeal abscesses, the tracheotomies, and even the tonsillectomies and adenoidectomies, which once filled the schedules of every hospital operating room—and often took place on the table of a farmhouse kitchen—had become endangered species. Today, ENT is just one of many players in the world of medical specialties.

American medicine is now in the throes of significant change which has displaced ENT from its premiere importance a half century ago. Although technology drives some of these changes, the revolutionary forces affecting the financing of medical care are exerting the most significant impact on the way physicians deliver and patients receive medical services. The HMO—Health Maintenance Organization—is a creature of these changes.

FIRST, SOME DEFINITIONS

The granddaddies and grandmommies of HMOs came into being more than fifty years ago, long before the term HMO was invented (which was during the Nixon administration). Some were cooperatives, such as the Group Health Association in Washington, D.C. Others were an amalgam of nonprofit health plans and for-profit physician corporations, such as Kaiser Permanente (of which my practice is a part). Both of these arrangements are now commonly, if not inappropriately, called staff-model HMOs. At the heart of these organizations is a physician group that contracts only with the HMO and provides services exclusively to HMO members. Historically the term staff-model was reserved for closed-panel HMOs, which hired physicians directly; the term group-model was used for closed-panel HMOs with self-governing, contracted medical groups.

More recently, as Medicare and state regulators have instituted prospective reimbursement schemes, "HMOs without walls" have developed. Such schemes include Independent Practice Associations (IPAs) and Preferred Provider Organizations (PPOs) and a host of newer amalgamations and hybrids which link physicians in their private offices to a common risk-sharing, prospective reimbursement pool.

HOW HMOs WORK

Consumers and providers respond to incentives in every marketplace. Here's an analogy: The consumer deciding between an indemnity plan and an HMO faces a choice similar to a hurried, hungry consumer shopping for a salad. The diner enters a restaurant offering two choices on the menu: a salad for $5.00 (it will be brought to the table promptly and comes on a big plate) or a $4.50 ticket to the all-you-can-eat salad bar (where the diner will get a small plate and may find a long queue). The incentives the restuarant is using will in part help the diner make his choice.

Here's where your career choice comes in: A risk-sharing pool of physicians (or a health plan employing salaried physicians) is like the management of the restaurant offering only an all-you-can-eat option. It has to be determined how the salad bar should be priced—and with what size plate and with how long a queue—to compete with the restaurant next door offering only table service.

Let me offer another analogy: You need some custom-fitted widgets for your home and your budget is tight. The widgets must meet certain quality standards, but you are not a particularly good judge of widget quality, nor do you have a lot of time to shop around. You know of two equally competent widgetmakers in the market, either of whom will come to your home to make them. One widgetmaker offers you widgets at a fixed price per widget, the other widgetmaker will work on site at a fixed hourly rate. What factors govern your choice of widgetmaker?

Now, turn the question around and think of yourself as the widgetmaker. What incentives do you perceive will govern your performance and that of your fellow widgetmakers? Such are the incentive questions governing HMO versus Fee-for-Service (FFS) care.

Ideally, the physicians in an HMO really work together. In the Kaiser Permanente model, for instance, the term pre-paid group practice (PPGP) is preferred over the more generic label, HMO. Many HMOs enjoy a culture that recognizes that collective efficiency is in the best interest of every physician member. Collective efficiency, furthermore, is achieved when each player in the team performs the role for which he or she is best qualified. When a PPGP is optimally functioning, the orthopedist sees only those cases of low back pain that need operative skills. And so, a truly successful HMO must define itself by the quality of the physicians it attracts and retains. As a young physician, your attractiveness to an HMO will to an ever-increasing degree depend on your willingness to remain an excited, enthusiastic team member, to share your expertise with your colleagues, and provide better health care to your patient population at a competitively affordable cost.

A CASE IN POINT

Let's consider the HMO practice of a primary care physician—a pediatrician, and her working relationship with a referral physician—an ENT specialist.

The Primary Care Physician's Role

Families make their decisions about health plans based on cost, location, and the reputation of the primary care physicians belonging to the plan. These physicians need to be caring and to be perceived as such—not that every physician shouldn't measure up to that standard! The primary care physician takes care of most of the patient's needs and, importantly, coordinates the care of the patient as the patient moves through the system receiving specialty care which the primary care physician herself cannot provide. In this sense she plays a public health and a personal physician role. The patient in the HMO depends on her to keep in mind the cost of tests and procedures and hospitalizations, for the more profligate she is in her decision making, the higher the costs are for the patient. At the same time, she must ensure that her patient receives the best care she and her colleagues can provide.

The primary care physician is supported in her role by telephone advice nurses who, under physician-designed protocols, manage many of the "worried-well" problems that do not require physician attention. She is also supported by nurse practitioners who, again under physician supervision but with considerable autonomy and the ability to prescribe a restricted range of drugs, greatly assist the doctor in routine care.

When the pediatrician needs a referral specialist—the ENT surgeon— she has access to one with whom she has already developed a working relationship. Should she be dealing with a child with recurrent earaches, she knows the threshold her ENT surgeon uses before inserting tympanostomy tubes. She knows that nonoperative options, if equally effective, are preferred since they are generally less expensive.

The Referral Physician's Role

Unlike his peers in fee-for-service practice, the HMO ENT physician has a greater chance to operate on patients who really need surgery. He is delighted to share with his referring pediatricians all the techniques he knows in nonoperatively managing children with recurrent earaches. He doesn't need to see children who are not in need of his surgical services. It is in his interest, in the referring physician's interest, and in the patient's interest for him to have established a solid teaching relationship with the primary care physicians with whom he works.

GROUP PRACTICE

PPGPs have historically been distinguished by being both pre-paid and group practice. The pre-paid attribute is becoming a less distinguishing feature as more care is delivered under prospective reimbursement schemes. HMOs, such as Kaiser Permanente, are having to emphasize their group practice attribute in marketing their services.

It is self-evident that a group practice depends upon attracting, nurturing, and retaining excellent physicians—without such collective excellence the group is doomed to failure. Group practice also enables those physicians to interact in a supportive environment. When, for example, 25,000 to 30,000 members are served by a single facility in which thirty to forty physicians of a dozen disciplines function, there are laboratory, radiology, and pharmacy services, and a dozen or so such facilities are linked with common computerized services, a powerfully effective system results.

With their increasing size, however, the tendency for impersonality to develop in group practice HMOs is a constant concern. Irrespective of payment mechanism, a group practice physician must strive—and can only strive—to emulate the best of independent physicians in building the one-on-one doctor-patient relationship. A group practice physician can equal but not surpass the best of independent physicians in this regard. Over the next decade consumers (or their governmental surrogates) will determine whether pre-paid group practice or pre-paid independent practice prevails.

COMPENSATION IN AN HMO

Physicians are recruited by HMOs at market rate. As soon as they are engaged, however, they become team players in a cooperative venture in which they are all managers with a financial stake. The result of this collective interdependence is that the extremes of income differential, which had been commonplace in the FFS world in the 1980s are compressed.

At their best, HMOs find a way to recognize merit where it exists. The retention of excited, enthusiastic physicians depends in part on the HMO's ability to recognize exceptional performance. Merit has many characteristics, of which teaching skill, patient satisfaction, and professional leadership are but three. Merit may be recognized with awards, cash, administrative promotion, or educational leave. However, continuing education is not just a matter of compensation; it's a matter of survival. An HMO draws on its own strength and on outside resources. Optimally, it should allow extended educational leave—sabbaticals—to those physicians who can construct a study program of benefit to the HMO as a whole.

Most HMOs cover their physicians malpractice insurance, professional license fees, medical staff dues, and related professional expenses. In addition, most have health and life insurance benefits and generous retirement plans. There is no "start-up cost" in opening a practice.

CHANGE AGAIN

At this writing massive changes in the American health care system are imminent. Almost certainly some form of standard benefit package with universal access will emerge, which will force health plans to compete more on quality than on price, on risk management, or on utilization review. Quality can best be provided by professionals who are excited and enthusiastic about their work.

It will be the challenge during the 1990s and beyond for successful HMOs to seek out the brightest and best of young physicians. I hope you may be among those qualified to join the best of your colleagues in the best HMOs.

PUBLIC SERVANT, M.D.: PHYSICIANS IN PUBLIC HEALTH

Joshua Lipsman, M.D., M.P.H.

"In doing what we ought we deserve no praise, because it is our duty."

—St. Augustine

All across the United States public health services are helping people and communities stay healthy and prevent disease. Doctors can play an important role in this system. It is an invigorating career where you learn, early on, that the community is your patient.

- In a crack house in inner-city New Haven, an addict shoots up with a clean needle and syringe; as a result he doesn't infect himself or his shooting partners with the human immunodeficiency virus, HIV.

- In a shack in a small community in rural Texas, three children under five years old are vaccinated against measles and so are protected from deadly brain infection.

- In Minneapolis a pregnant woman starts treatment for sugar discovered in her urine; she later gives birth to a healthy baby boy.

- An immigrant in Los Angeles takes a course in food handling, then opens a restaurant that passes health inspection and becomes very popular.

When I started medical school at the Albert Einstein College of Medicine, I didn't know exactly what kind of doctor I wanted to be. But soon I found that my extracurricular activities, which were related to topical issues in medicine, were as important to me as my medical studies. And so, while I was studying anatomy, physiology, biochemistry, internal medicine, pediatrics, obstetrics, and many other subjects imbued with idealism from these experiences, I chose family medicine for my residency because it offers broad training in health and illness as most people experience them.

THE BEGINNING OF A CAREER COMBINING SOCIAL ACTIVISM AND MEDICINE

I became active in the American Medical Student Association, where hands-on projects help students to understand the social context in which medicine is practiced. I volunteered with a national physicians organization to educate people about the adverse health effects of nuclear war. And I participated for an extended period of time in a project to improve the health of the community in the South Bronx, which was near my school.

During my residency training at a University of Minnesota-affiliated hospital in Saint Paul, I became aware of the social and political turmoil occurring in Central America. I became involved with efforts to educate the public and to raise funds to support the health care of the Central Americans whose lives were negatively impacted by the civil strife. I visited affected areas in Mexico and El Salvador, delivering medical supplies and assisting with health care and teaching. I became increasingly aware of the connection between what I would see in medical examination rooms and hospital wards, and what happens in homes, on the streets, in communities, and in the countryside.

Since Uncle Sam paid for me to go to medical school through the National Health Service Corps, in return I owed three years of medical service after my residency in a place lacking sufficient health care services. I chose the Pine Ridge Indian Reservation in southwestern South Dakota. My time there was personally and professionally very challenging; it made intense demands on my intellectual and emotional resources.

Native American Indians, particularly of the Great Plains, are among the poorest and sickest people in the United States today. Many of them have medical problems that are caused and/or aggravated by alcoholism, violence, despair, malnutrition, and poverty. The situation can be overwhelming—to patient and doctor alike. I came to understand in a very tangible way that doctors will continue to work in clinics and emergency rooms and certain communities will continue to suffer serious illnesses and injuries until the root of social and economic problems outside hospital walls and in community settings are addressed.

CHOOSING PUBLIC HEALTH AS A SPECIALTY

My experiences in medical school, in residency, and on the Indian reservation helped me to decide on a career as a public health physician. I recognized that the practice of clinical medicine and the interaction of the doctor and the patient, occurs in a social context that impacts clinical medicine significantly. I wanted to understand and to influence that social context. Public health, defined as "the fulfillment of society's interest in assuring the conditions in which people can be healthy" (from a 1988 report "The Future of Public Health," by the National Academy of Science's Institute of Medicine) was the ideal career choice for a physician with such goals.

This, of course, required me to take additional training. Many graduate schools of public health offer programs leading to master's degrees in Public Health (M.P.H.), with various areas of concentration, including epidemiology, maternal and child health, international health, health education, public health policy and administration, and public health nutrition. About half a dozen of the schools offer Master's degree programs for working professionals, which allow you to continue working while making periodic visits to the campus, submitting work assignments through the mail, taking approved courses locally for transfer credit and completing degree requirements over a two to three year period.

There are many other pathways to and through the field of public health for physicians, including residencies in preventive medicine that medical students can enter directly. Some nonadministrative work in public health includes providing services directly, program planning, or policy-making. Besides work in local, state, and federal governments, there are private sector opportunities in nonprofit and voluntary agencies. There are also opportunities in public health outside the United States.

While I was living and working on the Pine Ridge Indian reservation I enrolled in a program through the University of North Carolina at Chapel Hill, with a concentration in health policy and administration. My two six-week summer sessions in Chapel Hill were idyllic. It felt like a public health summer camp for grown-ups. Though I worked hard absorbing new skills and knowledge, the weather was beautiful and I found time to swim and bike almost every day.

FINDING A PLACE TO PRACTICE

Toward the end of my tour of duty on the reservation, I began to look for the most challenging public health physician position I could find. I accepted a position as the medical director and administrator of the city system of public health clinics with the Houston Department of Health and Human Services. I managed seven sites that saw several hundred thousand patients a year in prenatal and well-child care, immunizations, family planning, sexually transmitted diseases, and tuberculosis. In addition, I also maintained (and still have) a regular practice of clinical medicine, seeing patients one-to-one. It is important for me to continue a clinical practice to avoid getting "rusty," see what service delivery is like on the frontline of my agency, and maintain credibility with my physician colleagues.

After a period of time in Houston, I had the opportunity to work as the director of a department of health. Since 1991, I have been the director of the Alexandria Health Department, in the northern Virginia suburbs outside of Washington D.C.

My position has many positive attributes. I have a great deal of autonomy. The health department staff is competent and committed, which, of course, makes my work easier. The city government is sympathetic and supportive of public health. Though there is a sizable disadvantaged population in Alexandria—which is the primary recipient of department services—there is also enough community affluence and a fiscally prudent city administration to provide the means to make it possible to have a significant impact on Alexandria's public health problems.

Managing this department is like being the captain of a ship on a perpetual voyage toward an optimally healthy Alexandria. My work is varied. It includes such activities as:

- Reviewing the work of department staff for quality and efficiency
- Tracking trends and changes in public health and applying them to the care I provide
- Serving as a local public health advisor, attending meetings and writing reports
- Maintaining relationships with representatives of local, regional, and state government and other agencies, and the public
- Ensuring that public health laws and regulations are followed.

In my work I use the intellectual disciplines and methods of problem solving that I learned in medical school—and the many experiences I've had since. There is a hierarchy of levels of specificity for the specialties of medicine. Some doctors focus on a single organ, some on one type of patient, some on the health of families. My concern is the entire community.

FROM GOVERNMENT ISSUE TO NONPROFIT STATUS: A LIFE IN PUBLIC SERVICE

Peter Hawley, M.D.

"The reward of one duty is the power to fill another."

—George Eliot

Careers don't always move in straight lines. Sometimes they follow curving roads, making turns resulting from changing values as you mature and encounter unexpected opportunities. While in college, I never had any intention of going to medical school, instead I thought I would pursue a Ph.D. in microbiology. My uncle, a physician in my hometown, convinced me that I could be both a physician and microbiologist. Accordingly, I applied to medical school, was accepted, survived the rigors of medical education, and predictably entered a residency in anatomic and clinical pathology. I was sure that my career as an academic pathologist and microbiologist researcher was finally set.

Following the first course, after my residency, I entered the U.S. Army to fulfill a military obligation, and was stationed at the U.S. Army Medical Research Institute of Infectious Diseases, in Frederick, Maryland. I saw my time in the military as a necessary and unavoidable detour in my career; instead it was only the first turn of the curving road. The Army presented many opportunities which otherwise would not have been available to me, including the only chance I had to devote myself almost full-time to pure laboratory research. Although I had done some bench research, predominately in white-cell function during my residency, my time in the Army allowed me to spend three years concentrating on one area of research: tularemia (an infectious disease) and the cell-mediated immune system which protects against tularemia. This research time was relatively unproductive as measured by published papers, but it turned out to be vitally important in the development of my future career. Although the atmosphere of doing research is vastly different in the military than in most teaching institutions, it is relatively unencumbered with both the politics and committee work experienced in most medical schools.

The Army presented me with a second opportunity—the benefits were not obvious to me at the time. As a pathologist with a primary laboratory orientation, I was not especially interested in direct patient-care. Imagine my surprise and consternation when I found that, on my first weekend at Ft. Detrick, I was the only physician staffing the troop clinic and inpatient unit. I saw twenty patients on that first day; thank heavens for the skills of nurses who guided me through the complexities of direct outpatient care.

OUT OF UNIFORM—BUT STILL "IN SERVICE"

After my required three years in the military, I moved on to become the Director of Microbiology in the clinical laboratory at the Veterans Administration Medical Center (now the Department of Veterans Affairs) in Washington, D.C., where I stayed for nine years. In comparison to the military, civilian U.S. government service is a totally different world. The Department of Veterans Affairs, although providing absolutely vital medical care to our nations' veterans, is steeped in bureaucracy. Learning to not only survive but thrive in such bureaucratic systems was a skill that put me in very good stead later in my career.

There are some distinct advantages to this kind of employment, especially for younger physicians fresh from residency programs. Generally government salaries, although not competitive for senior physicians, are quite competitive for younger physicians. The opportunity to get established in a career without the financial burdens involved with opening a practice cannot be underestimated.

THE CAREER ROAD TAKES ANOTHER CURVE

I received a telephone call that would substantially reshape my career, and, in fact, my entire life. It was from a friend who was the medical director of the Whitman-Walker Clinic, a community-based clinic providing health services to gays and lesbians in the District of Columbia. He wanted to know if I would be interested in volunteering in the Gay Men's VD Clinic. I was always fairly open about being gay to friends and close co-workers, and excited about a chance to continue to use my clinical skills. I began volunteering to see patients at Whitman-Walker both on Saturdays and evenings. During my first few years I learned something that I had long suspected: homosexuals are tremendously discriminated against within the medical systems in this country. Very few practitioners know anything about homosexual lifestyles and the diseases associated with homosexuality.

After three years of volunteering at the clinic, the medical director left and I was asked to be the volunteer medical director. This was right at the beginning of the AIDS epidemic. In those early years, Whitman-Walker clearly saw it had an important role to play because of the huge preponderance of AIDS cases among gay men. We started a variety of medical, social support, and housing services for people with AIDS. Since we were one of the few clinics in the country providing these services, I was continually called upon to serve as an advocate for people with HIV infection in a very public way.

Four years into being the volunteer medical director, we realized that we needed a full-time medical director. Because I was president of the National Association of VA Physicians, and was unable to leave my job with the government, we hired an outside physician as medical director and I moved back to being a clinic volunteer. However, when a year later the new medical director left to pursue other career options, I decided to leave the government and become full-time medical director at Whitman-Walker, which I have done for the last seven years.

The exponential growth of the AIDS epidemic resulted in an exponential growth in the need for services. Whitman-Walker's medical program has grown from a staff of one to a staff of almost forty. Presently my job has so many facets that I can hardly keep them balanced. I am a clinician providing direct services to gays and lesbians with AIDS, as well as services for other health-related issues; an administrator running a multimillion dollar medical program; a researcher primarily investing time in AIDS-related medications; an activist concerned with discrimination against people with AIDS.

Looking back over my career, I find I am in a very different place from where I thought I would be, yet it is impossible to regret any of it. The curving road from an academic bench researcher to a clinician has not been so difficult: For job satisfaction, there is no comparison to working in the nonprofit sector. Although monetary compensation is less, the satisfaction of providing services that people desperately need and cannot get in any other place is immeasurable. Additionally, being an advocate for patients, particularly gays and lesbians, is a privilege and an honor. Working with volunteers, especially volunteer physicians, is a way of always being a teacher while always being taught. The staff of nonprofits are as committed as any staff I have ever worked with. After years of working, I've come to the abiding belief that good, sensitive health care is a right of all individuals in society, and that free access to this care is an absolute necessity.

WHAT ELSE YOU CAN DO WITH YOUR MEDICAL DEGREE: WORKING IN PRIVATE INDUSTRY

Lisa Egbuonu-Davis, M.D.

"A wise man makes more opportunities than he finds."

—Francis Bacon

CHAPTER 22

When asked to explain my career choices, the question, "but why don't you want to be a real doctor?" frequently comes up. This refers to the fact that I do not spend a large percentage of my time in direct patient contact. As vice president for the public and government affairs department of a biopharmaceutical company, I believe "real" doctors can and should work to improve the population's health in a variety of ways. I have chosen to do so via participation in the management of large public and private health care systems.

TRAINING WITH A PURPOSE

Early in my career, I planned to run public health systems—particularly those that target poor and underserved children. To that end, I entered a four-year combined degree program at Johns Hopkins, which allowed me to obtain both a doctorate of medicine and a master's of public health in epidemiology. Subsequently, I completed both a three-year residency in pediatrics and a Robert Wood Johnson Clinical Scholar Fellowship at the University of Pennsylvania. The fellowship was specifically designed to develop physicians as leaders in a variety of nonbiological areas. I chose to study outcomes research (quality of life and economic evaluation of health care interventions) and majored in health care management as part of a master's degree in business administration.

Simultaneously, I worked as a consultant to a state health department. This was a tremendous opportunity to participate in real program development. I contributed to a maternal and child health program that provided poor pregnant women and infants with an expanded package of medical and social support. The program included rigorous medical evaluation, treatment, and follow-up; outreach efforts (including visiting nurse services) for hard-to-reach populations; transportation; and counseling regarding housing, substance abuse, and other needs. All these have a major impact on the health outcomes of pregnancy, delivery, and early childhood.

Solving medical problems for the urban and rural poor requires a broad definition of medically necessary care. As a pediatric consultant,

I contributed to the development of the medical services guidelines, reimbursement packages, quality assurance, and a program evaluation plan. I was also responsible for provider recruitment. The program was very successful and has since been expanded to include more working-poor families without insurance. This type of program impacts the health of more mothers and children than I could serve in a lifetime of full-time pediatric practice.

HEALTH CARE IN THE PUBLIC SECTOR

My first full-time job was as director of a statewide program for children with special health-care needs. The program served children with severe chronic physical and medical problems—from congenital heart disease to sickle cell disease, and paid for evaluation and treatment services for children who met the medical and financial criteria. The department had a staff of 90 and a budget of over $20 million. An advisory council of medical specialists helped develop and promulgate treatment standards. All the academic pediatric medical centers in the state and many private practice pediatricians participated. While in this job, I had a general pediatric faculty appointment at a children's hospital supervising residents in a pediatric clinic once a week. However, most of my time was spent in administering the program and in developing new services and outcome measures. This included a program of expanded public health nursing for chronically ill adolescents and new child health surveys to document program impact. Was this the job of a "real" doctor? It was far from full-time private practice, but the job affected the medical and social environment for some of the most challenging pediatric patients in the state.

Typically, working in the public sector allows you to have a great deal of responsibility early in your career. This is a wonderful opportunity and challenge for new doctors who want to learn how to manage and motivate staff in relationships very different from classic physician/ staff roles. Most public health jobs pay less than private practice, but the difference in income between many public health jobs and pediatric practice is minimal. Public health is a rewarding career for those who want to make an impact on the care that large population segments receive.

CORPORATE MEDICINE—
PHARMACEUTICAL STYLE

After a brief period in public health, I faced dual career issues which made me consider relocating. An internist, who was also a former Robert Wood Johnson Clinical Scholar, suggested that I consider the pharmaceutical industry. I had never considered this industry and had no idea what roles physicians played in it. I soon learned that physicians participate in a variety of ways including conducting basic laboratory research on diseases and therapies; supervising clinical trials of experimental therapies; assisting in the development of marketing and educational programs for physicians, managed health care staff, and government agencies; and serving in a variety of management roles.

Since I had training in research methods, I was hired as a clinical research physician. Initially, I worked in oral antibiotics, reviewing clinical trial results for experimental agents and writing reports on adverse events (side effects) on marketed products. Although I learned a great deal, I found some of the work tedious. Subsequently, I utilized my health economics and outcomes research training to develop protocols (study designs) for quality of life and economic evaluation of investigational and marketed drugs for depression, cancer, and infectious diseases. This newly emerging field was interesting and technically challenging.

One special project which I participated in was a joint public/private partnership to promote maternal and child health. Because the local infant mortality rate was high, my company loaned my services for three months to a not-for-profit entity. This entity—working with state and local health departments—formed a three-year program to fund prenatal and pediatric medical care, case management, social support, and community-based educational services. This was both challenging and rewarding.

As in the public sector, my major interest in the private sector was in managing health care systems. Because general managers in pharmaceutical companies tend to have a marketing background, I pursued a series of assignments in marketing, including work as a sales representative, product manager, and managed-health-care-marketing manager. During this period, I was recruited for a higher level position by another company. In my current position, I supervise state government lobbying, policy development, community health affairs, issues management, employee communications, and media and customer relations. My department serves as a link between evolving health care reform policy and a changing pharmaceutical industry and as the key communications link between the company and all of our customers.

The connection between public health and technological advancements is critical. For example, *H. influenza meningitis* previously killed and/or disabled many children. My company developed and marketed an *H. influenza* vaccine, and the disease is now rapidly declining in the population. However, it will take joint efforts of public and private sectors to make sure all children are adequately immunized. This includes adequate funding for staffing in public health clinics and educational efforts to convince parents about the importance of vaccination. As a pediatrician in both public health and the biopharmaceutical industry, I continue to work to improve the health of children.

I believe that if you define a doctor as someone who touches the lives of patients and improves their health, then the career path I've chosen demonstrates that a physician involved in public health and/or private industry can have these positive impacts and indeed be a "real" doctor. Whether you're one-on-one with a patient, developing a new agent, educating your colleagues about a new agent, or administering a public health program—the result is the same: a more informed, better treated, and healthier population.

IN SEARCH OF PERSONAL SATISFACTION: CHANGING CAREERS IN MEDICINE

William Kenneth Payne, II, M.D.

"We know what we are, but know not what we may be."

—Shakespeare

There was a time when the choice of practice made during medical school was the path followed until retirement—and usually was centered on patient care. However, over the past 15 years, more and more medical students are not choosing patient care, and an increasing number of working doctors are changing their practices mid-career. In fact, career changes are not looked upon as failures, rather as people eager for the challenge of new opportunities.

Why do doctors change their area of practice? A number of factors come into play—and, as you'll see, they are varied:

- more time with family

- less stress in life

- freedom from bureaucracy

- impact of health maintenance organizations (HMOs) and closed independent practitioners associations (IPAs)

- high cost of malpractice insurance

The options for career changers are many, including: academic medicine, administration, medical research, military, management and recruitment, ethics, journalism and reporting, and volunteer services. Let's review each of these options.

ACADEMIC MEDICINE

Of course, this means you want to be a teacher. You will encounter a diverse group of students, including: medical students, residents, nurses, physician's assistants, and medical peers who desire your expertise. Depending on the teaching institution, clinical research activities are part of the package of responsibilities. You will need to consider whether or not you want to continue private patient care.

ADMINISTRATIVE MEDICINE

Pursuing administrative medicine means you no longer have patient contact, however you will have an impact on the outcome and decisions in evaluating patient care. Administrative medicine can involve the peer-review process, the review of procedures used by the various specialties in patient care, and making recommendations to improve patient-care cost-effectiveness. Working in administrative medicine can occur in a number of diffferent venues, such as insurance companies; hazardous industrial workplaces; disaster relief agencies; public health programs; government agencies, like Social Security, the National Institutes of Health, and Veterans Administration; hospitals and clinics, and state medical boards.

MEDICAL RESEARCH

Utilizing your medical knowledge, and concentrating that knowledge on solving medical problems in order to improve patient care defines medical research. It is labor intensive, and requires a tremendous amount of money, support, and patience.

MILITARY MEDICINE

Military medicine is practiced within the Armed Forces and offers a complete spectrum of medicine. Early in your military medical career you are involved in direct patient care; as you move up in rank, you will function more in an administrative capacity. This path in medicine is highly structured and disciplined, and can involve the care of military personnel and their dependents, members of congress and diplomats, the presidential staff and family, and care on the battlefield. The Armed Forces has its own medical school, research programs, pharmaceutical and equipment needs, private patient care programs, outcome units (hospitals, clinics, field units, and critiques), investigative units (pathology and forensic medicine units), and administrative units.

MEDICAL MANAGEMENT

Medical management occurs primarily in HMOs, IPAs, and Managed Care Groups, and focuses on physicians' services. As the link between the physician practicing within those organizations providing patient care and the corporate or ownership group, you determine and fulfill such needs as personnel, equipment and supplies, hospital and physician contracts, and high-tech services.

MEDICAL RECRUITMENT

The field of medical recruitment is concerned with locating practice opportunities and other jobs for physicians, and so requires extensive medical knowledge. In addition to frequent traveling, medical recruiters spend a great deal of time on the telephone and managing correspondence.

MEDICAL ETHICS

A medical ethicist is often involved at the crux of medical care, balancing patients' wishes, physicians' expectations, families' desires, and the moral-ethical obligations to life. Many ethicists work on multi-disciplinary teams to help shape decisions about care and outcome for critical patients. With people living longer, the ethicist requires a knowledge base of current medical practice, including experimental approaches to treating disease.

MEDICAL JOURNALISM AND REPORTING

Medical journalism and reporting can be pursued in print and nonprint venues: radio, television, cable, on-line services, newspapers, newsletters, and magazines. Your medical background will be essential in evaluating and delivering information about medical care and innovations.

VOLUNTEER MEDICAL SERVICE

Organizations that request volunteer services include the Peace Corps, American Red Cross, World Health Organization, overseas communities, state/local free health clinics, and missionaries. Volunteering physicians are customarily subsidized with a stipend by the organizations making the request.

A VARIETY OF CAREER CROSSROADS

After completing year one of my surgical residency, I realized that four to five years of training for the surgical approach to treating medical diseases was not what I wanted as a lifelong profession. And so, when I heard about a family practitioner who at times allowed young doctors to join his practice, I contacted him—and was welcomed with open arms. Unfortunately, I discovered that our styles of practice were different, and we had to end that relationship.

Interested in experiencing a different side of medicine, I entered the Armed Forces. I was stationed aboard an aircraft carrier as the assistant ship surgeon and had an opportunity to visit the Pacific Islands and the Far East. This provided me with a first-hand look at many of the exotic diseases I had studied in medical school. My responsibilities included sick call, teaching soldiers how to survive in combat when injured, and preventive medicine.

Several senior grade officers tried to convince me to make the service my career, but I declined. I decided to leave the Armed Forces and start a pediatric residency. After receiving board certification, I opened an office for private practice pediatricians, and kept it going for many years. But as the medical bureaucracy grew—and the office personnel escalated from a two-person office to a six-person office—I decided it was time for another career change. I no longer enjoyed going to the office or hospital, and private practice was no longer professionally rewarding. And so, I turned to administrative medicine.

As a disability evaluation examiner, I am involved with many interesting issues, including administrative approaches to evaluating medical care, incompleteness of medical records, and treating source statements unsubstantiated by objective findings. Career change can alter a practice lifestyle. It can provide you with more time off, sabbatical leave, insurance coverage of all types (medical malpractice, life, health, dental, vision, and disability), paid holidays, travel and study opportunities, resolution of paperwork, and pension and retirement packages. Change should yield you greater personal satisfaction. If given the chance, I would take the same journey with my medical career.

To make an effective career change you must be aware of what is going on in the medical community. Some of the things that affect medicine are subtle, others are obvious, but you alone determine if and when a career change is necessary. Economic loss is minimal with each career change and there is much to gain in making the change that has many potential satisfactions.

REFLECTIONS

PART 6

SHARING YOUR TIME WITH OTHERS— VOLUNTEERISM

J. Kevin Belville, M.D. and
Charles H. Epps III, M.D.

"Whenever the art of medicine is loved, there is also the love of humanity."

—Hippocrates

Volunteerism is an expression of the humanitarianism that is at the foundation of the medical profession. The spirit behind it is wanting to make a difference in people's lives, knowing there won't be a monetary reward. Many physicians give free care during their careers, but for some, being a volunteer in a project—whether local or international—is much more important. Some physicians have found the rewards of volunteering so great, they have dedicated their lives to it.

MAKING THE DECISION TO VOLUNTEER

Many organizations around the country—actually, throughout the world—are eager for medical volunteers: for both ongoing and emergency service. However, a number of practical considerations should be a part of your decision to become a volunteer:

- What kind of commitment can you make? This comes down to time—and money. Are you able to give one day a week? One day a month? How many hours? Can you spend an afternoon every other week in the local clinic? The more thought you give to the when and how of your volunteer activities, the more likely you will pursue them.

- The ideal time for longer, more involved projects is between different steps in your medical training: between medical school and residency, or just after residency. Some medical school curriculums and residencies allow for volunteer activities. Once you are board-certified, even more opportunities will arise, since many organizations won't accept volunteers who aren't board-certified.

- Where are you willing to go to volunteer your services? If you are unable to travel or give large blocks of time, then a community-based volunteer program is most practical for you. Your local medical society is a good source for finding such a program, or you might try contacting your local Rotary or Lions Club.

- If you want an international experience, there are lots of opportunities. Information on these is available from such organizations as the U.S. Agency for International Development, the American Red Cross, as well as religious organizations.

- What are the risks in volunteering? The work can be difficult, especially in third world countries. Most volunteer projects are in very needy areas, which means a flood of patients await the volunteer doctor's arrival. Often, medical facilities are lacking, which requires patience, resourcefulness, and a sense of humor.

- There are also health risks: malaria, typhoid, and yellow fever are prevalent in many parts of the world and hepatitis is common, due to poor sanitation and polluted water. Finally, there are "frustration" risks. Every project has at least a little red tape. Even with small volunteer projects, it's easy to get frustrated by administrative requirements. It may seem unusually arduous getting started. And completing a project may leave you saddened when you realize that there are so many more patients needing care, but who probably won't ever receive it.

- What do you want to accomplish? You can provide care, organize a project, or teach others. It all depends on your abilities and interests— and the needs of the organization with which you affiliate yourself. You might even consider inventing your own volunteer project—for instance, setting up a free clinic that indigent patients can use once a week.

TWO VOLUNTEERS' EXPERIENCES

Dr. Charles Epps began his volunteer activities as a medical student at Johns Hopkins in the 1980s:

I had always had an interest in public health and so I spent a summer in a Baltimore City Health Department venereal disease clinic for one of my clinical rotations. I also began to volunteer at a private venereal disease clinic, where I continued to serve until graduation.

When I moved to Washington, D.C., for my internship and residency training, I began to volunteer at the Whitman Walker Clinic, which offers free venereal disease treatment, mental health counseling, and substance abuse counseling to persons with HIV disease and AIDS. During the early years of the AIDS epidemic I was appalled to see the ignorance and prejudice displayed by my medical peers who, in many instances, refused to treat people with AIDS. As the epidemic spread, it became apparent that many persons were becoming blind from *treatable* conditions because of lack of access to care. I received a grant from Howard

University College of Medicine to purchase equipment to treat these patients. Four years later, I became the director of the Eye Health Center for people with AIDS—the first of its kind in the world. While volunteering for this service, I continued my private practice in ophthalmology.

While working to establish the eye center, I also became involved in governance at Whitman Walker. I was appointed to the board of directors and subsequently served as president, presiding over an organization with a ten million dollar budget, 200 employees, and 1,800 volunteers.

The people I have worked with during my volunteer activities are committed, compassionate, and display the values that drew me toward medicine as a career. Many high school and college students decide to become physicians after volunteering in a health care setting. If every physician donated his or her time to a service organization, and advertised that fact, the image of physicians in this country—and the health of our citizens—would be much improved.

Dr. Belville felt the pull of an overseas experience and found himself, at the end of his residency, in a third world country treating patients with eye diseases:

After residency, I stayed overseas for a year, traveling from country to country with a team of ophthalmologists, teaching and treating patients. I've worked all over the world as a volunteer and found it a tremendous learning experience, both medically and culturally. You learn, by necessity, "low-tech" medicine, and in the process, discover how resourceful you can be. Now that I'm in a full-time practice, I spend as much of my vacation time as possible working on projects in second and third world countries. I just completed a two-year project setting up a volunteer hospital near Haiti, where there was no eye care available.

The world needs volunteers. There are many impoverished people in the U.S. and throughout the world who have no access to health care providers. Millions suffer needlessly for lack of routine medical care. No matter what kind of practice you choose to pursue, there are needy patients who will benefit by it.

Many volunteer physicians have discovered there are few activities in life that are as personally satisfying. As a volunteer, you will often experience a unique gratification that can be spiritually rewarding. Most volunteers encounter that feeling over and over, sometimes retiring to do it full time. Most physicians understand that the wonderful gift of healing is meant to be shared with everyone, especially those who cannot afford it.

KNOWING IT'S THE RIGHT THING TO DO: ETHICS AND MEDICINE

Edmund Howe, M.D., J.D. and

Marian Secundy, Ph.D., A.C.S.W.

"If decisions were a choice between alternatives, decisions would come easy. Decision is the selection and formulation of alternatives."

—Kenneth Burke

Medical care continues to become more advanced and sophisticated, in terms of the ever-growing body of knowledge—as well as high-tech aids—doctors bring to their diagnoses. There are still many instances, however, where the singular judgment of the physician is the "defining moment" in a patient's care. And, there are some instances when a doctor is faced with what is considered an ethical dilemma. In fact, some of the technological advances that have occurred over the last few decades have provoked many complicated questions about patient care.

WHEN A DOCTOR FACES AN ETHICAL DILEMMA

An ethical dilemma exists when finding an answer or solution to an issue or problem involves making a choice among options—and ensuring that the choice is made in accordance with accepted principles of conduct. An example that quickly comes to mind because of the front-page headlines it continues to provoke is euthanasia: Although some doctors consider aiding in ending the life of someone suffering from a terminal disease is antithetical to physicians' training, others feel it can be the only morally "correct" action to take.

Because many doctors feel uncomfortable and unprepared to make certain decisions alone—or even in concert with a patient, a patient's family, or another colleague—increasingly, doctors are enlisting the help of medical ethicists. And in recognition of this need, many hospitals have instituted their own ethics committees with which their doctors can consult. In fact, some states require all hospitals have such committees.

As a result, doctors, patients, and/or their families who are confronted with issues they do not know how to handle can speak with someone with special training and expertise. In most instances, ethics consultants are religious advisors, philosophers, nurses, doctors, and/or social workers who have spent time studying ethics. Their role is to point out the pros and cons of a particular course of action and assist the "client"—the doctor and the health care team—in talking with the patient and/or family to better clarify situations that need resolving. The various points of view that ethicists hold differ from person to person, but they are supposed to be able to separate their emotions from their ability to think rationally and logically about a particular problem.

INCORPORATING ETHICS INTO
MEDICAL TRAINING

Medical students and other health care professionals can study ethics as a part of their training. In fact, you'll find both required and elective courses on ethics in medical school. Don't avoid them! It will be to your professional benefit to develop skills in analyzing problems and shared decision making in patient care. Situations you are certain to be presented with in medical school—and real life—include:

- A patient who is so ill that little or nothing can be done to reverse the course of the disease. Question: Should the doctor declare the situation medically futile even when the patient or his/her family requests the treatment to continue?

- Question: How much should the cost of treatment influence decisions about what and how much to do to treat a particular patient?

- Question: When resources are limited (e.g., intensive care beds, organs for transplantation), what should determine how they should be distributed?

- A couple wants to have a baby only so they can donate its brain tissue to a family member with Parkinson's disease. Question: Should the doctor continue caring for this patient?

PERSPECTIVES OF A MEDICAL ETHICIST

Dr. Edmund Howe is a psychiatrist, lawyer, and ethicist who has been called upon to advise doctors and families on a variety of different issues. Here he shares some of his and other ethicists' experiences.

Infant Management

I was away at a medical conference when I received an urgent call from the head of a hospital ethics committee on which I serve. She informed me that one of their patients—a baby—was dying. Because the parents believed a miracle could occur, they were insisting that all interventions that could prolong the baby's life be carried out. They were also demanding that the doctors stop giving the infant morphine to relieve its pain, because they believed that continuing the morphine would result in the baby's further deterioration.

According to my colleague, the medical staff was highly distressed, but felt there was nothing they could do. I told her I knew of no legal or ethical precedent permitting parents to tie the hands of doctors in this manner. And, in a case like this, child abuse statutes clearly support physicians' treating babies' pain over parents' objections. In addition, since the infant was already on a respirator, even if the morphine depressed its respiratory drive, it would not result in the child's death. So, I recommended that she call the baby's doctors and ask them to treat the baby with morphine at once, so that it need not suffer unnecessarily any longer.

Allowing Someone to Die

A young man with untreatable cancer, who had only six months to live, fell into a coma as a result of an infection. The best chance of treating the infection involved a surgical operation. The issue that confronted his doctor and family was whether to carry out this rather intrusive measure, knowing that if they did not operate he would die. The critical question they had to face was what the patient would want. His wife thought he definitely would not want the operation. His parents and siblings, however, believed that, since he was a "fighter," he would.

Although the ethics consultants knew that the customary approach, established by law, is to leave the decision to the spouse, they also understood that going this way could cause estrangement between the spouse and her husband's family. Since the law need not be the last word, the consultants asked the spouse to consider working toward a compromise with her family. This would bring them closer together and ensure that her child would be able to enjoy a rich relationship with his grandparents, aunts, and uncles after his father died.

As you can tell, there are seldom any "right" answers. Rather, the ethicist strives to arrive at the best—or better—solution for the particular problem, taking into consideration what is important to everyone involved. However, the final decision—which usually represents a compromise on the part of all involved—is always made by the doctor, the patient, or family.

THE CALL TO MUSIC: EARLY RETIREMENT FROM MEDICINE

Cleveland Francis Jr., M.D.

"There is no royal road to learning; no short cut to the acquirement of any valuable art."

—Anthony Trollope

O n April 1, 1993, I left the medical profession. I had practiced fourteen years as a cardiologist in Northern Virginia and was the president of a five-associate group known as the Mount Vernon Cardiology Associates. I retired from medicine to pursue a career as a country music singer. Many people asked me how I came to make such a decision. Let me try and explain.

It was atypical for many who grew up in southwest Louisiana to escape poverty, but somehow, with the help of a very strong-minded and persistent mother, my five sisters and I all received a higher education. We became involved in the teachings of the church at an early age. We all demonstrated some musical talent and three of my sisters became professional music educators.

As a child, I was very interested in the guitar and was fascinated by all the rich music of Louisiana: gospel, blues, cajun, country, and rhythm and blues. In fact, I made my first guitar out of a cigar box and window-screen wire. When I was nine years old, my mother, who had saved money for a year, bought me a twenty-five dollar Sears and Roebuck Silvertone guitar. It wasn't long after teaching myself to play, that I began performing. I became good enough to join a gospel quartet in high school as vocalist and guitarist. I also played the tuba in the high-school band, and served as student director of the high school chorus. My academic studies were also very important to me and while in high school I became very interested in the sciences. After graduation, I attended Southern University in Baton Rouge, Louisiana, and majored in premedical zoology. Jokingly, I've often said that I left my hometown of Jennings with three things: a science book, a bible, and a guitar.

MUSIC WAS NEVER FAR BEHIND ACADEMIC STUDIES

While at Southern University, my musical talents came to the attention of Dr. Huel Perkins, chairman of the music department. He encouraged me to continue to play and write songs while pursuing my pre-med major. From Southern University I enrolled in the College of William and Mary in Williamsburg, Virginia, for a master's degree in biology. While I was attending William and Mary I still found time to devote to music and became well-known in the local musical circles. Fans of my music contributed enough money so that I could record an album entitled "Follow Me."

My educational whirlwind continued. Upon completion of my master's program, I enrolled in the Medical College of Virginia in Richmond. While pursuing my medical degree, I continued to sing and write songs. During summer vacations, when most medical students worked in the hospital, I headed to local cafes and roadside bars, to play my music until the next school year. In 1963, I graduated from medical school and did my medical residency in Internal Medicine at George Washington University Hospital, in Washington, D.C. Despite a rigorous work schedule, I continued to perform albeit on a very limited basis. Once my residency was completed, I stayed on to enter a fellowship in cardiology.

At long last, I opened a solo practice in Alexandria, Virginia, and found myself with twenty-four-hour a day on-call responsibilities. After two years of dealing with this hectic routine, I added my first Associate— soon after that I added four more—making it possible for me to resume my music performances. Happily, these included charitable causes, such as an invitation to perform for Vietnam Veterans, writing a tribute to the late Dr. Martin Luther King, Jr., and writing a song on AIDS Awareness, which was performed at the World Health Organization and the International Red Cross. I'm also pleased by the thousands of dollars that were raised for cardiac patients, through a concert I performed for the American Heart Association.

MUSIC OVERTAKES MEDICINE AS A PASSION

My break came in 1991, as a result of treating a patient who had suffered a massive heart attack. My patient (who recovered without complication), had a brother who was a professional musician living in Florida. When he heard about my music, he asked for samples of my work. Impressed, he introduced them to an independent record producer. He, too, was impressed—and asked me to record an album! It was a dream come true: I traveled to Nashville, and recorded the album, "Last Call for Love." One of the songs, "Lovelight," soon ranked nine on the Country Music Television Charts! Events moved swiftly, as I signed a multi-album contract from the next release, "Tourist in Paradise," which sold over one hundred thousand copies! Between the national press coverage, videos, and personal appearances, I had little time for my medical practice. But I knew it was in good hands with my associates.

The press was now referring to me as the "Singing Cardiologist," a title I was never fond of, since it did not describe my love for both medicine and music. As proud as I am of my musical accomplishment, I am also proud of my accomplishments in medicine: I started a major medical group from the ground up, and practiced medicine with the same vigor that I had for the music. I gained the respect of the community, colleagues, and my patients. I was extremely proud to be a physician.

But there was never a time when music was not part of my life and I reached a point where I knew that with the increased demands of both professions, I would have to decide whether I could—or should—do both. I wondered if I had the right to leave medicine. Did I have an eternal obligation to this discipline to practice until retirement, or death, whichever came first? Were medicine and music equal in importance? How could I give up the security of the medical profession for a career in the performing arts? I consulted my close friends but this would be an answer that could only come from me.

Too many people let themselves become consumed by their profession and lose the true essence of themselves. This is particularly true for physicians. In our Western culture, life has a value second to none and since physicians are directly involved in the care of life, we have been given a very high standing in society. I somehow kept Cleveland Francis, Jr., M.D., and Cleve Francis, poet and musician, separated. Dr. Francis, with the long, white coat and stethoscope hanging around his neck, commanded respect from his patients, hospital, office staffs, and colleagues. On the other hand, Cleve remained the man from rural Jennings, Louisiana, who grew up in poverty and first played his music on a homemade guitar.

As far as most of my patients were concerned, my national reputation as a musician was not perceived as infringing on my attention to their medical issues. I can only recall one patient who switched to one of my associates because he wanted a doctor who was only committed to medicine. I respected his decision, but it reminded me of a belief I hold dear, which is that we are individuals first—our job titles are mere add-ons.

I have tried to see my job as being a caregiver. My task was to do everything possible to improve my patients' quality of life. Equally important, however, was the effort to maintain my own quality of life. I feel strongly that my involvement in music helped me succeed at both tasks and improve the lives of the people I have cared for as patients.

Through luck, circumstances, and a lot of perseverance, I am realizing my dreams. I have given up the financial security that I enjoyed as a doctor, but I feel that I am on the right track with my music. Becoming a major country star is high on the horizons.

Two Healing Arts: Religion and Medicine

Martin W. Gallagher Jr., M.D.

"No one can give you better advice than yourself."

—Cicero

It was a quiet, crisp October morning. Finding a parking place along Reservoir Road at eight in the morning is a real task. Today was the first day of anatomy class. Imagine, by the end of next semester, we will know the anatomy of the entire human body. I was walking up the driveway between the Emergency Room and side entrance of the medical school when panic set in: "Why in God's name am I doing this? Most people my age are already established in careers, have children, own a house. And I need to know the entire anatomy of the human body in seven months! Am I crazy? My God, I'm forty-one years old!"

I stopped, took a deep breath and thought, "Today, I only need to learn the arm."

Four years later, after celebrating the baccalaureate mass for the graduates at Holy Trinity Church, and giving the invocation at the commencement ceremony at the Kennedy Center, I heard my name called and walked up onto a stage to receive my diploma as a Doctor of Medicine. I had graduated, by no means at the top of the class, but I had graduated from Georgetown University Medical School. The elation was, well, a great feeling.

HOW DID THIS COME TO BE?

In 1956, about one year after the Korean War ended, I was a bright-eyed freshman on a scholarship at Georgetown University as a pre-med major. But distracting me from pre-medical studies were deep stirrings to become a priest. Because ours was a very Catholic family, second-generation Irish immigrants, it was difficult for me to be the oldest of seven, with twelve years of parochial education, and not think about becoming a priest once—or twice. And that's what I did.

Entering the Jesuit order with the goal of ordination to the Catholic priesthood is a lengthy process, involving thirteen years of training before ordination, and two more years of training after that. In 1969, Lawrence Cardinal Sheehan, Cardinal Archbishop of Baltimore, performed the rite of ordination on our group of about fifteen candidates at Woodstock Theological College near Ellicott City, Maryland.

MEDICINE BECKONS

A few years later I met the director of oncology nursing at Georgetown Nursing School. We shared many conversations about cancer, death, and dying, and I became interested in the hospice movement. At that time Georgetown University Hospital was setting up a hospice unit, in conjunction with Blue Cross/Blue Shield, to see if it was an economically feasible alternative to caring for dying patients in a nonhospital setting. One day the director suggested that if I were to get involved in hospice, medical training would help me understand the entire patient situation better. I agreed. Shortly thereafter, I was enrolled in a nighttime nursing program at the University of the District of Columbia.

Two years later, with an associate arts degree and a nursing license in hand, I began working as a registered nurse at Georgetown University Hospital. It was quite interesting. Reunited with several of my former high school students from Georgetown Preparatory School where I taught as part of my Jesuit training, who were now attending physicians, soon the idea was reborn: become a doctor. This time, I went the distance. My way was paid when I was accepted into National Health Service Corps. All I had to do was give back three years of service some time after residency, in an underserved area of the country.

Not surprisingly, I was one of the older residents in the Internal Medicine program at the Washington Hospital Center, in Washington, D.C. It was a good program with lots of ICU/CCU experience. Cardiac catheters were done on selected patients, many of whom were flown in from out-of-town. This was the leading-edge of modern medicine, and it was great to be a part of it. Medstar, the shock-trauma unit, was a marvelous experience that gave me the confidence, as a third-year resident, to run a major resuscitation effort and being in charge of the team doing so.

A PRIEST-DOCTOR PRACTICE

Payback for medical school training came in 1986. After a prolonged process of being assigned to a region of the country by the National Health Service Corps, and then negotiating within that area for a position, I finally ended up in an area of the country many people never imagined exists: Cut off, Louisiana, some sixty miles south of New Orleans, in true bayou country.

It was fun being a doctor and priest in this all-Catholic area of Louisiana. Besides being medically underserved, there was also a shortage of clergy. I would often let one or another of the solo priests take a Sunday off, and do mass and preach. The parishioners, many of whom became my patients, sort of enjoyed the whole thing.

My homing instinct is strong, and so the middle Atlantic became the target of the search for opportunities after my "time" was up down south. Hagerstown, Maryland, a small community ringed by mountains, seemed very attractive. I had tired of beltways and interstates and the prospect of doing rounds in three or four city hospitals during day-time traffic was abhorrent. The local hospital (one hospital!) had just begun recruiting physicians for hospital-sponsored practices, since many of the older physicians in the community were not recruiting replacements. A bold start was made with the initiation of an OBGYN practice to care for indigent mothers. There was a gradual evolution, and other specialties in primary care were started. Thus we were assembled, internists, family practice doctors, and surgeons.

This has been the life of an older medical student. What next? Law school at seventy!

WANTING IT ALL:

MEDICINE AND

FAMILY

Rodney L. Ellis, M.D. and

Caryl G. Mussenden, M.D.

"Vision: It is essential for survival. It is spawned by faith, sustained by hope, sparked by imagination and strengthened by enthusiasm. It is greater than sight, deeper than a dream, broader than an idea."

—Charles Swindoll

CHAPTER 28

It is certainly advantageous to know early in life what career you want to pursue; we both had that privilege as children. Especially in the 1950s and '60s, it would bring smiling approval from our parents and others when we answered, "A doctor," to the question, "What do you want to be when you grow up?"

EARLY CHOICES

Rodney: "As long as I can remember—and this goes back to about age five or six—I wanted to be a doctor. But the reason why changed over time. Very early on, I wanted to make a lot of money and drive a big car like all doctors seemingly did back then. In high school and college, I developed a humanitarian mission, and wanted to make a difference in people's lives; medicine seemed ideally suited for this. By the end of my medical training, I looked at medicine as a noble profession that not only was intellectually rewarding, but that provided a role for me in society that would always be useful."

Caryl: "I don't know why at the age of six I wanted to deliver babies—maybe it was the influence of my physician father; maybe it was the pact I made with my twin sister that she would take care of the babies I delivered. Regardless of the reason, from an early age I was oriented to becoming a physician and never wavered from my goal. In retrospect, I feel it was a blessing, because the choices I made before getting to medical school were "preordained," for example, I knew I needed good grades to pursue a career in medicine."

CHOOSING STRUCTURED LIVES

In reflecting back, with such a clear and early commitment to becoming physicians, we developed a single-mindedness that willed us to do what was necessary to reach that goal. For both of us, the timing and selection of our first marriages were largely influenced by the rigors of medical school and residency. The exploration of our inner persona and happiness in relationships was not as important as having stability in our social lives in order to have the energy and willpower to complete medical training.

Caryl: "When you choose to become a physician, it is important to realize that in addition to achieving a comfortable lifestyle, your life will be rather structured. Especially during your medical training, you will have to forego nonacademic activities in order to study; your dating will be circumscribed; and committing to a steady relationship will be difficult. Whether in medical school, residency, or a newly established private practice, you will be so busy that only your studies, the demands of your practice, or the need for sleep will be at the top of your priority list.

I married a recent medical school graduate at the end of my second year, after we had been dating exclusively for three years. I thought I would be too busy for socializing, so at the tender age of 21, and probably too young for it, I got married. At 23, I was a senior medical student when I became pregnant with my first child. Fortunately, I was blessed with an uncomplicated pregnancy, and so lost no time because of sickness. Being married and having a child during a medical career will always be a challenge. I often felt torn between studying for final board exams, spending time with my daughter, and working on my marriage to a resident physician.

In some ways, being married to another physician is like being married to anyone else who has a busy, time-consuming career: Time for communicating can suffer, as can the relationship. My marriage was strained by the same sort of issues other couples with busy lives face: lack of finances, lack of time for each other, young children, and poor communication. If the marriage is not nurtured appropriately, everything else in the family can become strained.

It is difficult to know when the best time is for marriage. I do believe that couples must prepare themselves spiritually and mentally before entering into such an important commitment. What each partner expects in terms of the relationship, home life, children, child-rearing, and long-term goals, should be discussed in depth."

Rodney: "The day after I graduated from college in June 1970 at the 'wise old age of 21,' I got married. Within two weeks I moved to Palo Alto to attend medical school, and by October 1971, my first child was born. It's fair to say that things were happening rapidly in my life, although I don't remember feeling particularly anxious or rushed. Indeed, I remember explaining to a classmate's mother, who protested that my early marriage was premature, that I needed to marry so that I would not have to 'worry about dating during medical school.' As I focused on completing my preclinical courses during the second year of medical school, I took in stride, without deep reflection, the significance (if not gravity) of my wife's pregnancy and the birth of my son. She had taken a position in personnel administration at the medical school's hospital, and the pregnancy and her maternity leave all seemed to go smoothly.

As it turned out, we had different attitudes and feelings about child rearing which became apparent and were amplified by my daughter's birth in 1977. A number of incompatibilities (which seen in retrospect could probably have been prevented by a longer and more reflective courtship) revealed themselves over the years. In 1980, my marriage ended.

It is said that with each ending there is a new beginning, and it was at this point that my life became less structured and open to new choices, new changes."

PRACTICE CHOICES

In the late 1970s it was still relatively unusual for a newly trained physician to select a health maintenance organization (HMO) for a career. Private practice, while generally more demanding of time and effort, was attractive since it was generally more lucrative and certainly more prestigious. The overwhelming majority of practicing physicians, both nationally and locally, disliked even the idea of an HMO, and looked at HMO physicians with some disdain.

For very different reasons, in 1979 we both joined Group Health Association (GHA), the oldest urban HMO in the country, and at that time, the largest in Washington, D.C. We met in 1980, both recovering from unhappy marriages and looking to make the most of our choices in the field of medicine. HMOs were frequently unstable in those years, and GHA itself had suffered a divisive struggle, ending in the physicians forming a union during 1977–1978. GHA, however, provided a relatively certain base from which we were able to launch our medical careers.

Rodney: "During Internal Medicine residency at Johns Hopkins hospital, I developed an interest in pursuing a career in primary care within an HMO for idealistic reasons: to have no concern about the patient's ability to pay for needed procedures and tests, to have a financial incentive to keep people healthy rather than to have reimbursement linked to treating an illness, and to have little or no worry over office and personnel management.

I quickly and enthusiastically immersed myself into the workings of the HMO, joining the Quality of Care Committee, helping to define and regulate the role of physician assistants/nurse practitioners, and giving educational workshops for patients—for which I gladly volunteered."

Caryl: "From the beginning of my residency, I needed a live-in housekeeper to be a surrogate parent for my children. Before finding the woman who has been with me for 15 years, I went through five people in a two-year period. Needless to say, this was stressful. For a short time after a foreign housekeeper walked out, the children had to come home on the school bus to an empty house. They would call me immediately and be home for about an hour before I would arrive. I am so glad those days are over! There is no question that this type of stress negatively impacted both the time I spent with my patients and children.

I had always envisioned myself in a private practice, but since I was a single parent and needed a steady income and stable practice hours, I joined Group Health Association, where I became one of 18 OBGYNs, taking calls two to three nights a month. I didn't have to worry about the business aspects of the practice, I didn't have to hire and fire staff, and I was home with my children most evenings. The negative aspects of GHA were that the physicians were unionized and I could only see GHA members as patients, which excluded many women outside of GHA. The lack of continuity of care also left a lot to be desired."

CHOOSING NEW DIRECTIONS

Yes—we met at GHA and we fell deeply in love. A physician-to-physician relationship has many potential advantages. Not only does it allow for professional discussions and sharing of work experiences, but an understanding of the demands of the career allows for a deeper level of support. Finally, there is a certain camaraderie as health care professionals share common friendships with other physician colleagues.

As our relationship matured and culminated in our marriage in 1983, we experienced freedom in thought and vision. We credit the happiness and security of our relationship to our willingness to explore self-development courses, spirituality, and new professional practice options.

Caryl: "At the end of two years at GHA, it was clear that I still hadn't found my career niche. The practice environment at GHA was not as structured as I wanted, so I felt it was time to move on. When the offer of a position in a large group private practice came along, I accepted: It was more in line with my aspirations. I became the first woman doctor in a five-man OBGYN practice. Even though I was still an employee, I was able to see women who were not members of an HMO; I was not restricted to whom I could refer my patients; and I saw all of my own patients.

A few years later, I decided it was time to go into private practice. The idea of striking out on my own was made more attractive because of the security that my husband provided as a salaried physician at GHA. Founding a private practice is difficult, yet in the long run very satisfying. You must consider a number of factors, including: the amount of start-up money needed, the location of the office, securing and maintaining staff, what salaries to pay, how to attract clientele, outfitting the office, what supplies are needed, and so on.

As I see it, the main advantage of owning your own practice is that you get to call the shots. I structured my office the way I wanted it, in every aspect. The downside is that as a solo practitioner, you are on call 24 hours a day. My practice kept me away frequently from my new spouse and two small children."

Rodney: "I obtained broader perspective as I approached my mid-thirties, such that even though I had become a bit of a champion for the HMO cause, I had no deep philosophical problem with my wife pursuing an independent fee-for-service practice. Quality of care and the doctor-patient relationship became more important to me than the structure of the delivery system. However, a number of factors did become sources of conflict and dissatisfaction for me in regards to GHA.

Early on, I noted that as employees, unless there was an unusual dedication to professionalism and patient care, physicians attracted to HMOs often had a '9:00 to 5:00' mentality and looked forward to having the least number of patients and problems disrupt that schedule. Further, the 'doctor's union: management' equation did not map well onto the 'doctor:patient' and 'physician:broker of health care resources' equations. There were distinct shortcomings in incentives for physicians to be responsible health-care team leaders, certainly required in any successful health-care system. In addition, there seemed to be a growing conflict between corporate bottomline needs and patient care needs.

Despite nine years of tenure, with positions of growing responsibilities, I resigned from GHA in 1987. I decided to open my own practice, feeling confident that with the experience of helping my wife begin hers, and the security of her successful practice as a base from which to launch mine, I would succeed."

HAVING AND RAISING CHILDREN: FEW CHOICES

Since a physician marriage can easily be strained by the demands and stresses of the job, it is very important to discuss each other's views about responsibility for the home, children (to have or not have), child care, and child rearing. We have always considered our four healthy children to be a supreme blessing in our lives. As physicians acutely aware of what can go wrong from "in utero" through young adulthood— and beyond, both physically and psychologically, we appreciate the health and successful upbringing of our four offspring. Yet the obligate need to spend quality time with them has been the most persistent challenge of our lives as busy medical practitioners.

The responsibility in raising children is awesome: They learn by what they see and feel from those around them, giving prime importance to parents as child rearers. Combine a two-doctor marriage, each spouse with two children, and each set of children with other parents who have their own households, agendas, and philosophies, and you have a truly complex situation.

It is probably true that the love and concern we have for our children is so unlimited, that combined with the challenges and pitfalls facing today's kids, we will always feel we have not done enough for them. Yet, we continue to look forward to each day's challenges, as we are so richly rewarded by our children as they grow and develop.

AFTERWORD

"The price of greatness is responsibility."

—Winston Churchill

Many years of rigorous training transforms the person into the physician. But what is a physician? Healer. Intellect. Technician. Teacher. Advisor. Leader. Clinician. Researcher. Administrator. Entrepreneur. A physician is all this and much more.

Physicians are knowledgeable about many things, but we put this knowledge into practice one patient at a time. The challenge is in the individual approach required for each person's unique circumstance. We care about the quality of patients' lives and hope that our intervention will improve their lives. This doctor-patient relationship is special and very unique: We are advocates for our patients. Because physicians can have significant influence over patients, it is not a relationship to take lightly.

We are a part of other relationships, too. We are members of families, and so involved with our family's health. Many of us are small businesspeople and are concerned with the health of our employees. We are members of the larger community and so are concerned about the health of society: We worry about persons with disabilities, the young, the old, the poor, minorities, and women who are disproportionately affected by lack of access to health care.

In this age of health care reform we are concerned about the health care delivery system and its impact on our ability to provide quality care for our patients. In our unique position as doctors, we move the health of the nation forward. We hope to have this positive impact on reform of the health care delivery system.

As physicians we hope to inspire the next generation, especially women and minorities, to enter the profession. We want to be your mentors and role models. By sharing our experience and insight, we hope you can see your goal more clearly.

If after reading these pages you chose to embark on a medical career path, we applaud your decision. Commitment and persistence will see you through the many stages of the process. Though it is a challenging road to follow, you will experience a lifetime of rewards.

ABOUT THE CONTRIBUTORS

CONTRIBUTORS

J. Kevin Belville, M.D., is a full-time staff ophthalmologist with the Capital Area Permanente Medical Group in Kensington, Maryland. He also is a volunteer medical consultant to the International Eye Foundation in Bethesda, Maryland. Dr. Belville has worked as a volunteer ophthalmologist for many overseas projects.

Deborah L. Bernal, M.D., is a board-certified specialist in physical medicine and rehabilitation. A graduate of Howard University College of Medicine, she did her residency and fellowship training in Sinai Hospital of Baltimore, and Johns Hopkins University School of Medicine. Dr. Bernal is in private practice in Silver Spring, Maryland, and serves as chair of the Young Physician Section of the Medical Society of DC. She also enjoys an academic affiliation with Howard University College of Medicine.

Charles W. Carpenter is director of financial aid at The George Washington University School of Medicine and Health Sciences in Washington, D.C. Mr. Carpenter manages and administers all federal, state, institutional, and private financial assistance programs.

Benjamin S. Carson Sr., M.D., is director of pediatric neurosurgery at Johns Hopkins Hospital. Over the last few years he has developed, along with the plastic surgery division, a significant craniofacial program in which children with congential deformities undergo combined neurosurgical and plastic surgical reconstructions. He is the recipient of over 200 honors and awards, including fourteen honorary doctorate degrees, serves on several professional boards and committees, and continues to teach as associate professor of neurological surgery, oncology, pediatrics, and plastic surgery.

Lisa Egbuonu-Davis, M.D., M.P.H., is a board-certified pediatrician, earning both her medical degree and Master's in Public Health from Johns Hopkins University. Dr. Egbuonu-Davis also earned an MBA from the Wharton School, University of Pennsylvania, receiving the Kaiser Award in Health Care Management. Dr. Egbuonu-Davis currently serves as Vice President, Public and Government Affairs for the Lederle Laboratories and Lederle-Praxis Biologicals divisions of American Cyanamid Company. She resides in New Jersey with her husband and daughter.

Rodney L. Ellis, M.D., and *Caryl G. Mussenden, M.D.,* practice Internal

Medicine and Obstetrics-Gynecology respectively, sharing offices in D.C. and Virginia. Deeply involved in antidelinquency efforts, medical politics, and other community and church activities, they are also raising four children and a foster child as they reside in McLean, Virginia.

Charles H. Epps III, M.D., is an Ophthalmologist in private practice in Washington, D.C. Dr. Epps also serves as director of pediatric ophthalmology at Howard University Hospital and as a consultant to the Hospital for Sick Children and Kendall Elementary School at Gallaudet University. He has volunteered at Washington, D.C.'s Whitman-Walker Clinic since 1984, and is also director of the clinic's eye health center for persons living with AIDS.

Cleveland Francis Jr., M.D., is a native of Jennings, Louisiana. He attended Southern University, the College of William and Mary, and the Medical College of Virginia, where he received his medical degree. Dr. Francis served as president of Mount Vernon Cardiology Associates and director of cardiac rehabilitation, chairman of the department of medicine, director of the coronary care unit and vice-president of the Mount Vernon Hospital medical staff. Cleve Francis will release an upcoming album in August, which features a duet with singer Patti Austin.

Martin W. Gallagher Jr. M.D., is an internist in a multi-specialty hospital-sponsored practice in Hagerstown, Maryland. He was ordained a Roman Catholic priest in the order of the Society of Jesus (Jesuits), became a registered nurse, and started Georgetown University School of Medicine in 1979, at the age of 41.

Peter Hawley, M.D., became the full-time Medical and Laboratory Director of the Whitman-Walker Clinic—and recently renamed the Elizabeth Taylor Medical Center-Whitman-Walker Clinic, the largest AIDS service organization in the national capital area, in 1987. After attending the State University of New York Upstate Medical Center and receiving his M.D., he completed a residency in Anatomic and Clinical Pathology. For his work with people with AIDS, Dr. Hawley became one of the Washingtonians of the Year for 1985.

Edmund Howe, M.D., a professor of psychiatry, is director of The Program in Medical Ethics at the Uniformed Services University Health Sciences, in Bethesda, Maryland. A member of six ethics committees, he also serves as editor-in-chief of *The Journal of Medical Ethics.*

James R. Hughes, M.D., is a full-time pediatrics doctor in the inner city of Washington, D.C., where he is employed by the Capital Area Permanente Medical Group. A 1960 graduate of Harvard Medical School, Dr. Hughes has enjoyed caring for children in academic, fee-for-service group practice, solo, staff model HMO, and pre-paid group practice environments. He joined Kaiser Permanente in 1979. The views he expresses in his article are his own and do not necessarily reflect those of Kaiser Permanente.

Renee R. Jenkins, M.D., is professor of pediatrics and child health, and director of adolescent services in the Department of Pediatrics and Child Health at Howard University College of Medicine, in Washington, D.C. She received her pediatric training and adolescent medicine fellowship training at Albert Einstein College of Medicine, Montefiore Medical Center, New York. She was certified in pediatrics in October 1976.

Robert I. Keimowitz, M.D., is dean for academic affairs, and professor of medicine and health care sciences at The George Washington University School of Medicine and Health Sciences in Washington, D.C. The views expressed in *Making the Cut: Getting into Medical School* are the authors, and do not necessarily reflect those of the University or its Medical Center.

Ruth Kevess-Cohen, M.D., a graduate of Harvard College and the Johns Hopkins University School of Medicine, is a primary care physician practicing internal medicine and geriatrics in Silver Spring, Maryland. Her activities include teaching residents, interns and medical students; making house calls for home-bound elderly; visiting patients at nursing homes and assisted living facilities; serving on hospital and medical school committees; and consulting on quality assurance. In November, 1993 she was the subject of the *Washington Post*'s Sunday magazine cover story, "Doctor of the Future." She is married and the mother of three children, 10, 7 and 3.

Peter E. Lavine, M.D., is a board-eligible Orthopedic surgeon, practicing in the Washington, D.C. area. His medical degree and residency training was performed at Georgetown University Medical Center. He was fellowship trained at the University of Bern, Switzerland. He is clinical instructor at Georgetown University Hospital, George Washington University Hospital, and A.O. North America.

LaSalle D. Leffall Jr., M.D., F.A.C.S., is professor and chair of the Department of Surgery, Howard University College of Medicine. He is a surgeon, oncologist, medical educator, and leader in professional and civic organizations. His professional life has been devoted to the study of cancer, especially as it affects African-Americans. A recipient of numerous awards and honors, Dr. Leffall also is a diplomat of the American Board of Surgery and fellow of the American College of Surgeons and the American College of Gastroenterology.

Joshua Lipsman, M.D., is the director of the Alexandria (Virginia) Health Department. A Fellow of both the American Academy of Family Physicians and the American College of Preventive Medicine, Dr. Lipsman is board-certified in family practice and in public health and general preventive medicine. He is on the voluntary medical school faculty of Georgetown University and The George Washington University.

Lawrence S. McDonald, M.D., graduated from medical school when he was 41 years old. Currently, Dr. McDonald is involved in AIDS care and medical ethics and also teaches at local medical schools. He states his thanks to his family and friends for their support, and to the staid New England dean who "contributed greatly to my opportunity to become a doctor."

William K. Payne II, M.D., is a board-certified pediatrician. He has experienced many career changes, from family practitioner, assistant ship surgeon, school physician, public health clinic physician, emergency room physician, and membership on the Governing Board of a 275-bed hospital. Currently, Dr. Payne serves as medical consultant for the State of California, Department of Social Services as a disability evaluation examiner for federal programs.

Vivian W. Pinn, M.D., is associate director of the National Institutes of Health for Research on Women's Health. She has served on the faculties of Harvard Medical School, Tufts University School of Medicine, and Howard University School of Medicine, where she was professor and chair of pathology.

Catherine L. Salem, M.D., is a board-certified Radiation Oncologist practicing and teaching at Georgetown University. She completed her internship in 1985 at Aultman Hospital in Ohio and a residency in 1988 at Case Western Reserve Hospital in Cleveland, Ohio. Currently, Dr. Salem is Assistant Professor of Radiation Oncology at Georgetown University Medical Center.

Marian G. Secundy, Ph.D., is a professor and director of the Program in Medical Ethics, Howard University College of Medicine, Department of Community Health and Family Practice. A practicing family therapist, she served as co-chair of the Work Group on Ethical Foundations of the New Health Care System in Hillary Rodham Clinton's Health Care Task Force.

Luette S. Semmes, M.D., trained in both internal medicine and dermatology at the Washington Hospital Center, in Washington, D.C. Her internal medicine practice experience is limited to "moonlighting" at several hospitals in the D.C. area and volunteering at several free clinics while completing a dermatology residency. Presently, Dr. Semmes practices in Salisbury, Maryland, where she limits her practice to dermatology.

Kevin R. Smith, M.D., is a facial plastic surgeon in Houston, Texas. He completed a fellowship in facial plastic surgery in Birmingham, Alabama following a residency in Otolaryngology at the University of Texas (Houston). Currently he is an assistant clinical faculty member in the department of Otolaryngology at the University of Texas Medical School at Houston and serves as a special advisor to the Dean of the Medical School for the Project 3000 by 2000.

Nancy L. Snyderman, M.D., has served as medical correspondent for "Good Morning America" since 1987, reporting on a wide-range of topics affecting both men and women. Dr. Snyderman is an associate clinical professor of Otolaryngology—Head and Neck Surgery, at the California Pacific Medical Center and the University of California, San Francisco.

Duane J. Taylor, M.D., is currently involved in the full-time practice of Otolaryngology, Head and Neck Surgery and Facial Plastic and Reconstructive Surgery in the Metropolitan D.C. area. He is a graduate of the combined B.S./M.D. program from the University of Akron and the Northeastern Ohio Universities College of Medicine. Dr. Taylor began his practice with the Capital Area Permanente Medical Group in 1991 and currently serves on the Board of Governors for the American

Academy of Otolaryngology Head and Neck Surgery.

Ronald Tinsley, M.D., specializes in Ear, Nose, and Throat surgery which he has practiced in Fairbanks and Juneau, Alaska. Before settling in Alaska, where he has lived for over 20 years, Dr. Tinsley graduated from Meharry Medical College in Nashville, and completed his internship at Hurley Hospital in Flint, Michigan, and residency in Baltimore, Maryland. Dr. Tinsley is a native of Illinois.

Maria L. Chanco Turner, M.D., is a board-certified dermatologist where she is Medical Officer of the Dermatology Branch at the National Institutes of Health, in Bethesda, Maryland. Dr. Turner graduated from the University of the Philippines College of Medicine, and completed a residency at Yale University Medical School.

APPENDIX A

Choosing a Residency

Ethics and Medicine

Getting into Medical School

Medicine and Family Life

Medicine as a Transportable Career

Medicine Is a Business

Minorities in Medicine

Pre-medical Preparations

Public Health Physician

Specialty Boards

Volunteerism

Women in Medicine

A P P E N D I X A

CHOOSING A RESIDENCY

American Medical Association
Accreditation Council for Graduate Medical Education (ACGME)
515 North State Street
Chicago, IL 60610
312-464-4920
(Provides a directory of requirements and programs for each residency program, also called the "Green Book.")

Council of Medical Specialty Societies
P.O. Box 70
Lake Forest, IL 60045
(708) 295-3456
(Provides publication, "Choosing a Medical Specialty," which lists residency programs, and other information and data on current specialties.)

ETHICS AND MEDICINE

Uniformed Services
University of the Health Sciences
4301 Jones Bridge Road
Bethesda, MD 20814
301-295-3293
(Provides information on courses on ethics.)

GETTING INTO MEDICAL SCHOOL

Association of American Medical Colleges
2450 N Street, NW
Washington, DC 20037
202-828-0400
(Publishes "Trends in Medical School Applicants and Matriculants," covering 1978 through 1994, and *Medical School Admissions Requirements.*)

MEDICINE AND FAMILY

American Medical Association
Alliance Department
515 North State Street
Chicago, IL 60610
312-464-4920
(Provides general and support services information to physician spouses.)

MEDICINE AS A TRANSPORTABLE CAREER

"Social Transformation of American Medicine." Basic Books, Inc., 1982. New York, NY

MEDICINE IS A BUSINESS

American Medical Association
Practice Management Department
515 North State Street
Chicago, IL 60610
1-800-366-6968
(Provides information on co-sponsored seminars related to starting a practice; answers questions on practice-related concerns for statewide physicians.)

MINORITIES IN MEDICINE

Association of American Indian Physicians
1235 Sovereign Row, Suite C-7
Oklahoma City, OK 73108
405-946-7072
(Provides information on statewide network programs.)

Association of American Medical Colleges
2450 N Street, NW
Washington, DC 20037
202-828-0400
(Publishes the *AAMC Manual*; also a listing of publications related to career opportunities for minorities in medicine.)

"Directory of Financial Aids for Minorities." Schlachter, G.A. 1993-1995. (Provides names of over 2,200 scholarships, fellowships, loans, grants, awards, and internships for black, Hispanic, Asian, and Native Americans. Write to: Reference Service Press, 1100 Industrial Road, Suite 9, San Carlos, CA, 94070.)

Epps, A.C., and Pisano, J.C., Med Rep at Tulane: "Effectiveness of a Medical Education Reinforcement and Enrichment Program for Minorities in the Health Profession" 1985. Future Publishing Co., Inc., 2 Belford Ridge Rd., Mt. Kisco, NY 10549.

"Searching, Teaching, Healing: American Indians and Alaskan Natives in Biomedical Research Careers." Hailer, B.H., and Myers, R.A. (For copies, write to: Future Publishing Company, Inc., 2 Bedford Ridge Road, Mount Kisco, NY 10549.)

"Financial Aid for Minorities in Health Fields." 1993. (For copies, write to: Garrett Park Press, P.O. Box 190, Garrett Park, MD, 20896. Minimal cost.)

Interamerican College of Physicians and Surgeons
1101 5th Street, NW, Suite 502
Washington, DC 20005
202-467-4756

"Minority Physicians: A profile." U.S. Department of Health and Human Services; Public Health Services; Health Resources and Services Administration; Bureau of Health Professions; September, 1993.

National Institutes of Health
Office of Minority Affairs
9000 Rockville Pike Building 1, Room 260
Bethesda, MD 20892
(800) 272-4787 or 301-496-6095
(Provides information on admission requirements.)

National Medical Association
1012 10th Street, NW
Washington, DC 20001
202-347-1895
(See article on African-American 'firsts' in academic and organized medicine, compiled by Charles H. Epps Jr., M.D., in *Journal of the National Medical Association*, Volume 85, No. 8, 1993.)

National Medical Association
National Minority Mentorship Recruitment Network
1012 10th Street, NW
Washington, DC 20001
202-347-1895
(Provides information on mentoring for women and minorities.)

National Medical Fellowships, Inc.
254 W. 31st Street
New York, NY 10001
212-714-0933
(Provides information on career opportunities and financial aid for minority students.)

Office of Statewide Health Planning And Development
Health Professions Career Opportunites Program
1600 Ninth Street, Room 441
Sacramento, CA 95814
916-653-0730
(Provides several booklets: "Career Choices: Health Professions Opportunities for Minorities"; "Financial Advice for Minority Students Seeking an Education in the Health Professions"; "Minorities in Medicine: A Guide for Premedical Students"; and "Time Management for Minority Students." No cost.)

PRE-MEDICAL PREPARATIONS

American Medical Association
515 North State Street
Chicago, IL 60610
312-464-2400
(Provides vital information on pre-medical planning in *Journal of the American Medical Association*, Volume 268, No. 9, September 2, 1992. Minimal cost.)

Association of American Medical Colleges
(Membership and Publication Orders)
2450 N Street, NW
Washington, DC 20037-1129
202-828-0400
(Provides publication, "Trends in Medical School Applicants and Matriculants," summarizing demographic characteristics and selected academic qualifications of medical school applicants and matriculants. Latest copy available for years 1983-1994.)

PUBLIC HEALTH PHYSICIAN

American College of Preventive Medicine
1015 15th Street, NW, #403
Washington, DC 20005
(202) 789-0003

American Medical Student Association
1890 Preston White Drive
Reston, VA 22091-5430
(703) 620-6600

American Public Health Association
1015 15th Street, NW, 3rd Floor
Washington, DC 20005-2699
(202) 798-5600

SPECIALTY BOARDS

American Board of Medical Specialties
1007 Church Street, Suite 404
Evanston, IL 60201-5913
(708) 491-9091, (708) 328-3596, FAX
(Provides information on specialty board requirements and certification
process.)

VOLUNTEERISM

American Red Cross
National Headquarters
1730 E Street, NW
Washington, DC 20006-5399
202-737-8300
(Provides information on national and international volunteering.)

International Eye Foundation (Check with your local ophthalmological
chapter for address and phone; provides opportunities on international
projects for volunteer ophthalmologists.)

Lions Club (Provides opportunities for local volunteering. Check local
yellow pages for an office.)

The Rotary Club (Provides opportunities for local volunteering. Check
local yellow pages for an office.)

U.S. Agency for International Development (AID) (Check with your
local Medical Society for address and phone number; provides information on international volunteering.)

WOMEN IN MEDICINE

American Medical Association
Women in Medicine Services
515 North State Street
Chicago, IL 60610
312-464-2400

"Women's Health Issue." *Journal of the American Medical Association*, Vol 268, No. 14, October 1992.

American Medical Women's Association
801 North Fairfax Street
Alexandria, VA 22314

"Gender Equity in Medicine." *Journal of the American Medical Women's Association*, Vol. 48, September/October 1993.

Association for Women in Science
1522 K Street, NW, Suite 820
Wasington, DC 20005

Association of American Indian Physicians
1235 Sovereign Row, Suite C7
Oklahoma City, OK 73108

Association of American Medical Colleges
2450 N Street, NW
Washington, DC 20037
(Publishes a directory of women in medicine specialty organizations; provides *1994 Publications Catalog*, which lists medical school curricula, descriptions of medical schools, admission requirements, opportunities for women and minorities in U.S. medical schools and their faculties, and medical specialty choices.)

Bickel, J. and Quinnie, R. *Building a Stronger Women's Program: Enhancing the Educational and Professional Environment.* Association of American Medical Colleges, Washington, 1993.

From, J.D., Bickel, J. and Jones, R.F. *Faculty Affairs in Academic Medical Centers: A Selected Annotated Bibliography.* Association of American Medical Colleges, Washington, 1992.

Sherman, E.A., Johnson, D.P. and Whiting, B.E. *Participation of Women and Minorities on U.S. Medical School Faculties 1980-1990.* Association of American Medical Colleges, Washington, 1990.

Smith, V.D. and van der Veen, P. *Trends in Medical School Applicants and Matriculants: 1981-1990.* Association of American Medical Colleges.

Association of Women Surgeons
414 Plaza Drive, Suite 209
Westmont, IL 60559
(Publishes "Pocket Mentor: A Manual for Surgical Interns and Residents, 1993.")

"Women's Health Issue." *IM-Internal Medicine*, April 1994.

"Women in Surgery." *Archives of Surgery*, Vol. 128, June 1993.

Women Scientists and Engineers Employed in Industry: Why So Few?
   National Research Council, National Academy Press, Washington,
   1994.

National Medical Association
National Minority Mentor Recruitment Network
1012 10th Street, NW
Washington, DC 20001
(Provides information on mentoring for women and minorities.)

APPENDIX B

Federal Loan Programs

Federal Perkins Loan

Federal Stafford Loan

Federal Unsubsidized Stafford Loan

Health Education Assistance Loans

Primary Care Loan

MEDLOANS Alternative Loan Program

MEDCAP Medical Alternative Loan

Exceptional Financial Need Scholarship

Financial Assistance for Disadvantaged
Health Profession Students

National Health Service Corps Scholarship

National Health Service Corps Loan
Repayment Program

APPENDIX B

FEDERAL LOAN PROGRAMS

Federal Perkins Loan Federal Perkins Loans are authorized under Title IV of the Higher Education Act and administered by the individual medical schools.

Amount: Need based. Up to $5,000 per year, depending on other aid awarded. Payable in at least two disbursements.

Fee: None.

Interest: Fixed rate of five percent.

Eligibility: Must complete and submit a need analysis application (FAFSA). Must have unmet need after deducting the expected family contribution from the budget. Also must make satisfactory academic progress as determined by the individual medical school.

Grace Period: Six months after leaving the institution or finishing an authorized internship/residency deferral.

Repayment: Monthly principal and interest payments begin after the grace period (as shown above). A borrower may have up to ten years to repay. The minimum monthly payment is $50.00. No prepayment penalty. Shorter repayment periods are available at the borrower's request.

Federal Stafford Loan (formerly GSL) Federal Stafford loans are authorized under Title IV of the Higher Education Act and administered by the Department of Education.

Amount: Need based. Up to $8,500 per year, depending on other aid awarded. Payable in at least two disbursements.

Fee: Origination fee of five percent to cover the administration costs. Guarantee fee of up to three percent.

Interest: Variable rate of up to nine percent. Federal government pays the interest while the borrower is enrolled in school.

Eligibility: Must complete and submit a need analysis application (FAFSA). Must have unmet need after deducting the expected family contribution from the budget. Also must make satisfactory academic progress as determined by the individual medical school

Grace Period: Six months after leaving the institution.

Repayment: Monthly principal and interest payments begin after the grace period (as shown above). A borrower may have up to ten years to repay. The minimum monthly payment is $50.00. No prepayment penalty. Shorter repayment periods are available at the borrower's request.

Federal Unsubsidized Stafford Loan Federal Unsubsidized Stafford Loans are authorized under Title IV of the Higher Education Act and administered by the Department of Education. Effective July 1, 1994, the Federal Unsubsidized Stafford Loan replaces the old Supplemental Loan for Students (SLS) program.

Amount: Up to $10,000 per year, depending on other aid awarded. Payable in at least two disbursements.

Fees: Origination fee of five percent to cover the administration costs. Guarantee fee of up to three percent.

Interest: Variable rate of up to nine percent. Interest accrues while the borrower is in school.

Eligibility: Must complete and submit a need analysis application (FAFSA). Must have unmet need after deducting the expected family contribution from the budget. Also must make satisfactory academic progress as determined by the individual medical school.

Grace Period: Six months after leaving the institution.

Repayment: Monthly principal and interest payments begin after the grace period (as shown above). A borrower may have up to ten years to repay. The minimum monthly payment is $50.00. No prepayment penalty. Shorter repayment periods are available at the borrower's request.

Health Education Assistance Loans (HEAL) The HEAL program, administered by the Department of Health and Human Services, ensures commercial rate loans for health professional students.

Amount: Need based. Up to $20,000 per year, depending on other aid awarded. Payable in at least two disbursements.

Fees: Six percent insurance premium (dependent upon the medical school's HEAL loan default rate).

Interest: Variable rate of up to three percent above the 91-day Treasury Bill rate and adjusted quarterly. Interest accrues and can be compounded up to every six months while the borrower is in school and in deferral. (Note: Because there is an 18 percent interest or higher rate cap for HEAL loans, it is generally recommended that students use the Federal Stafford and Unsubsidized Stafford before taking a HEAL loan.)

Eligibility: Same as Federal Stafford Loan. Exception: Must be a citizen or a permanent resident with an unrestricted I-151 or I-551 card (Green Card).

Grace Period: Nine months after leaving school or finishing an authorized residency deferral.

Deferral: Up to four years for internship/residency training. An additional three years for borrowers who complete a residency in family medicine, general internal medicine, general pediatrics, or preventative medicine and who are practicing in one of these primary care fields.

Repayment: Monthly principal and interest payments for up to ten to twenty-five years (terms dependent on total HEAL debt). Graduated repayment option (smaller payments in early years) is available. No prepayment penalties. To avoid excessive compounding and higher debt burden, borrower should make some payments, if possible, while still in residency deferral.

Primary Care Loan (formerly HPSL) The Primary Care Loan Program is a low interest rate Title VII loan that is funded by the Department of Health and Human Services for health profession students.

Amount: Total tuition charges plus $2,500. Payable in at least two disbursements.

Fee: None.

Interest: Fixed rate of five percent.

Eligibility: Must have unmet need after deducting expected family contribution from the budget. Also must make satisfactory academic progress as determined by the individual medical school. A recipient must sign a contract and agree to enter a residency in family medicine, general internal medicine, general pediatrics, or preventative medicine and practice in that primary care field until the loan is repaid or be considered in breach of the contract. Such action will cause twelve percent interest to be assessed on the total loan from the original disbursement date until the time of the breach of contract. The borrower will then repay the entire loan amount within three years.

Grace Period: Twelve months after leaving institution. Must be used prior to any deferment periods.

Deferral: Up to four years for residency training.

Repayment: Monthly principal and interest payments begin after any deferment period (as shown above). A borrower may have up to ten years to repay. The minimum monthly payment is $50.00. No prepayment penalty. Shorter repayment periods are available at the borrower's request.

MEDLOANS Alternative Loan Program (ALP) The MEDLOANS ALP program, offered through the Association of American Medical Colleges (AAMC), extends commercial rate loans for health profession students attending medical schools.

Amount: Up to $20,000 per year, depending on other aid awarded.

Fee: Seven percent insurance premium at origination with an additional two percent added at the time repayment begins.

Interest: Variable rate of up to 2.7 percent above the 91 -day Treasury Bill rate prior to graduation and 2.85 percent after graduation. The interest rate is adjusted each quarter. Interest accrues while the borrower is in school and in deferral.

Eligibility: Same as Federal Stafford Loan. Exception: Must be a citizen or a permanent resident with an unrestricted I-151 or I-551 card (Green Card). Credit checks are performed to determine eligibility.

Grace Period: Three to four years after leaving school or finishing an authorized residency deferral.

Deferral: Not applicable.

Repayment: Monthly principal and interest payments for ten to twenty years (terms dependent on total MEDLOAN debt). Graduated repayment option (smaller payments in early years) is available. No prepayment penalties. To avoid excessive compounding and higher debt burden, borrower should make some payments, if possible, while in residency.

MEDCAP Medical Alternative Loan (MAL) The MEDCAP MAL program, offered through Norwest Bank, extends commercial rate loans for health professions students attending medical schools.

Amount: Up to $20,000 per year, depending on other aid awarded.

Fee: Five percent premium at origination with an additional two percent added at the time repayment begins.

Interest: Variable rate of up to 2.5 percent above the 91 -day Treasury Bill rate prior to graduation and 2.85 percent after graduation. The interest rate is adjusted each quarter. Interest accrues while the borrower is in school and in deferral.

Eligibility: Same as Federal Stafford Loan. Exception: Must be a citizen or a permanent resident with an unrestricted I-151 or I-551 card (Green Card). Credit checks are performed to determine eligibility.

Grace Period: Three years for authorized residency training.

Deferral: Not applicable.

Repayment: Monthly principal and interest payments for ten to twenty years (terms dependent on total MEDCAP debt). Graduated repayment option (smaller payments in early years) is available. No prepayment penalties. To avoid excessive compounding and higher debt burden, borrower should make some payments, if possible, while in residency.

Exceptional Financial Need (EFN) Scholarship This program provides funds for students who demonstrate exceptional financial need.

Amount: Full tuition and fee charges.

Eligibility: Must complete and submit a need analysis report. The program is designated for medical students who demonstrate extremely low personal and family resources on the need analysis report. Limited funding available: only the most needy students receive awards. All recipients are required to complete a primary care residency within four years of graduation and to sign a contract indicating a commitment to practice primary care medicine for a period of five years after the training period. Primary care is defined as family medicine, general internal medicine, general pediatrics, or preventive medicine. Failure to honor the commitment causes the total scholarship monies plus an appropriate interest rate to be due and payable within three years after the breach of the contract to the Department of Health and Human Services.

Repayment: None.

Financial Assistance for Disadvantaged Health Profession Students (FADHPS) This program provides funds for students who demonstrate exceptional financial need. Also, the students must come from an educationally or economically disadvantaged background.

Amount: Full tuition and fee charges.

Eligibility: Must complete and submit a need analysis report. The program is designated for medical students who demonstrate extremely low personal and family resources on the need analysis report. Limited funding available: only the most needy students receive awards. All recipients are required to complete a primary care residency within four years of graduation and to sign a contract indicating a commitment to practice primary care medicine for a period of five years after the training period. Primary care is defined as family medicine, general internal medicine, general pediatrics, or preventive medicine. Failure to honor the commitment causes the total scholarship monies plus an appropriate interest rate to be due and payable within three years after the breach of the contract to the Department of Health and Human Services.

Repayment: None.

National Health Service Corps (NHSC) Scholarship NHSC scholarships are extremely competitive. Only a limited number of scholarships are offered on a national level. Two-, three-, and four-year scholarships are available for medical school students.

Basic Info: Acceptance at an AMA or AOA approved school of medicine in the United States or Puerto Rico; U.S. citizens with a willingness to practice primary care medicine in medically underserved areas. Benefits: Up to four years of tuition and fees; authorized books, supplies, and equipment; monthly stipend for the year

National Health Service Corp (NHSC) Loan Repayment Program

NHSC Loan Repayment program was authorized under Public Law 100-177 in December, 1987. Repays qualified government and commercial educational loans incurred for a health professions education in return for a set service commitment period.

Basic Info: U.S. citizenship; limited to health professionals who are in practice or postgraduate training; students who are in their last year of a health professions institution. Benefits: Can repay up to $120,000 for four years of service for all qualified government and commercial educational loan.

INDEX

To

VITAL SIGNS

Mentors
  for minority women, 47
  to stimulate motivation, 21
  for women, 45
Merit, characteristics of, 116
Military medicine, 126, 137
Minority groups. See also specific
  minority
  admission to medical schools,
    29
  choosing medical specialty,
    35–36
  doctor-patient relationships, 36
  history of, in medical school,
    32
  peer relationships, 36, 37
  premedical preparations for,
    33–34
  surviving racial encounters in
    medical school, 34–35
Morehouse Medical College, 33
Motivation, stimulating, 21–22

National Board of Medical
  Examiners, 63
National Health Service Corps.,
  159
National Hispanic Mentor
  Recruitment Network, 47
National Institutes of Health,
  working at, 110
National Medical Association, 35,
  47
National Minority Mentor
  Recruitment Network, 47
National Residency Matching
  Program, 71
National Student Medical
  Association, 35
Native Americans
  medical problems of, 121
  percentage in medical field, 32
Nonprofit sector, medical career in,
  127–128

Novello, Antonia, 32
Nurse, duties of, 99–100

O

Office manager, duties of, 99
Office planning, 99
Outcomes research, 130

P

Pain, treatment of infant's,
  149–150
Part-time practice at HMO,
  108–109
Patient-doctor relationship in
  primary care versus medical
  specialties, 87
Penicillin, discovery of, 112
Perkins, Huel, 152
Personal relationships
  and location for medical
    practice, 104, 106
  strain of medical career on,
    83–84
Personnel
  hiring and retaining, 99–100
  office, 99
Pharmaceutical industry, careers for
  physicians in, 132–133
Physical strength, need for, in
  medicine, 10
Physician
  clinical research, 132–133
  commitment to becoming, 162
  primary care, 114–115
  referral, 37, 115
Physicians union, 164
Preferred Provider Organizations
  (PPOs), 113
Pre-paid group practice (PPGP),
  114, 115